THE MISSISSIPPI METHODISTS

1799-1983

A Moral People "Born of Conviction"

Ray Holder

MAVERICK PRINTS
1984

Copyright © by Ray Holder 1984

Library of Congress Cataloguing in Publication Data

Holder, Ray
The Mississippi Methodists
1799-1983

Endnotes: p.
Index of Persons

1. Mississippi—history, culture, politics.
2. Methodism—polemics, division, unification.
3. Slavery—abolitionism, proslavery activists.
4. Race—racial images, rights, blacks, Indians.
5. Education—intellectual concerns, institutional advances.
6. Biographical—leadership profiles, moral postures.
I Title

ISBN 0-9612932-0-9 (Cloth)
    0-9612932-1-7 (Paper)

Manufactured in the United States of America

First Edition

Contents

For

*Young Mississippians
bending resolutely to
unfinished tasks.*

The Mississippi Methodists

Prolog and Acknowledgments

Ride on, blessed Redeemer, until all states and nations are subdued unto thy sacred way.

Francis Asbury

Mississippi, this southern enclave of romance and realism we natives cherish as "home," has emerged as a conspicuous showcase for writers of international reputation. They have laid bare her soul and moral character before the critical eyes of the world, lauded her "sense of place" and her "heroes," anathematized her demagogues and "closed society," and idealized and denigrated her serried struggle for societal acculturation and racial sanity across two centuries of history.

Yet, with the exception of Richard Aubrey McLemore's substantial chronology of the Baptists to 1970, no recent overview of any religious body in this state and its moral and cultural impact upon the commonwealth has appeared in print. Thus the student, the historian, and the general reader is virtually denied access to crucial chapters of The Mississippi Story without which our understanding of the past is essentially defective. For that reason I am prompted to submit these brief chapters to the reader.

I feel that the time is ripe to tell something of The Methodist Story, beginning in 1799, when not a single Wesleyan adherent was known to have settled within four hundred miles of Natchez, to the Bicentennial of American Methodism being celebrated during 1984-1985. During those eighteen decades an evangelically aggressive people survived every conceivable social ill from slavery to fratricide while reaching out with new life to the mounting populations of Alabama, Louisiana, western Tennessee, the

Florida Panhandle and eastern Texas. With modest pride the Mississippi Conference can lay claim to the title, "Matriarch of Methodism in the Deep South."

I am also prompted to address, as objectively as a Mississippian is capable, the "racist" image which my Methodist friends have painfully borne since abolitionists unleashed their Juggernaut upon slaveholders early in the 1830s. Indeed, as late as November 1982 a Methodist official of Global Ministries in New York publicly upbraided his Mississippi brethren for their "racist attitudes." Of this, also, I have by virtue of my roots been roundly arraigned during thirty years of ministry in two great urban melting pots, one on the West Coast, one in the Midwest. Little did my arraigners realize that as a barefooted lad in the piney woods near Old Salem Campground I literally cringed at the sight of church stewards and deacons parading down mud-rutted Main Street vested in white sheets illuminated by a flaming wooden cross. As a "city-priest" I was later to think "How mild! My neighbors merely signed covenants excluding 'those people' from the purchase of homes within their parish bounds."

Even so, not a few of my Anglo-Catholic peers were convinced that calculated racial discrimination in any corner of this land of the free would surely have aroused the moral conscience of John Wesley whom the Anglican Communion now venerates as a saint. I am here insisting that his American disciples of every race are today, in large measure, men and women of no lesser moral stature, and that Mississippians who now gather in unsegregated councils of their church and communicate at the same altar side-by-side are essentially no exception. They strive to become One People "born of conviction," and "bending to the task" of healing the wounds of a fractured world which Mr. Wesley claimed as his "parish."

My task of gathering notes for these pages was

made far easier by librarians and archivists who welcomed to their stacks and manuscript collections a stranger in a round collar seeking *Methodist* materials. I am much obliged to those gracious men and women at Duke University, Yale University, Boston University, Drew Theological Seminary, Vanderbilt University, Emory University, the University of Chicago, Garrett Theological Seminary, DePauw University, the University of Southern California, Southern Methodist University, Louisiana State University, the University of Mississippi, Mississippi State University, Mississippi Department of Archives and History, and Millsaps College. Ecumenical courtesies were aplenty, and equally appreciated.

I am especially indebted to John Buford Cain and his daughter, Loyce McKenzie, for placing valuable manuscripts at my disposal from the Methodist Archives, Millsaps-Wilson Library. Laura Drake Satterfield Sturdivant enthusiastically shared with me obscure letters of Alexander Talley and Benjamin Michael Drake. Robert L. Ezelle spent precious time orienting me on forces at work shaping the Methodist course of action during the difficult decades of the 1950s through the 1970s. Clyde C. Clark seemed delighted to fill me in on the finer nuances of "conference politics" in recent years. Ross Henderson Moore read a preliminary draft of the manuscript and, thankfully, quietly suggested that his former pupil might profitably apply a sharp red pencil to certain passages.

Without the careful eye and clement soul of my wife, Virginia, whose father was one of Wilbur Fisk Tillett's "boys" at Vanderbilt, my *faux pas* would of a certainty have filled a much larger volume of old-fashioned *errata*.

Ray Holder

The Feast of John and Charles Wesley, Priests
3 March 1983

One: Beachhead at Natchez Under-the-Hill

Ours has been a sort of spiritual cavalry dash—winning one field after another in rapid succession and sending down the lines the shout of victory.

Charles Betts Galloway

In the spring of 1799 Mississippi settlers celebrated their first anniversary as a territory of the young Republic. Sometime near that April day a canoe in tow of a flatboat edged onto the muddy bank of the Natchez Landing.[1] A wayworn stranger wearing a coonskin cap and a tattered version of a round-breasted coat stepped ashore at the end of a "lonely and mysterious" odyssey from Charleston, South Carolina, *via* the Cumberland River. Clutching his Bible, the Methodist *Discipline* and a bundle of evangelical tracts from the pens of John Wesley and other Oxford dons,[2] Tobias Gibson limped to a nearby tavern alive with the sound of fiddlin' and festivity. There, with the bar as his altar and barmaids and stevedores as his sheepish flock, he offered his first prayer on Mississippi soil.

This scene, of course, is part fact and part fancy. The man who established the Wesleyan beachhead at Natchez Under-the-Hill left no diary or journal for historians to examine.[3] Yet from oral sources collected by his immediate successors it is reasonable to assume that the newcomer then trudged up the steep bluff in search of lodging, possibly at the tavern operated by David Michie, conveniently located near a livery overlooking the river.[4] After securing a horse to replace the one he had exchanged for a canoe on the Cumberland, Tobias rode six miles to Washington, the capital of the territory, and

1

apparently preached in the open like his idols, John Wesley and Francis Asbury.

From there he made his way up the Natchez Trace to the home of his cousin, Randall Gibson, who had migrated to "The Natchez" during the Spanish regime.[5] Randall had married Harriet McKinley (McKenly), purchased a small contingent of slaves, and was engaged in a modest plantation operation. If he had not been informed that his cousin was on his way to the territory, he was undoubtedly surprised, and pleasantly so, when Tobias rode up to the barn. Tobias, however, was unpleasantly surprised to learn of his cousin's recent conversion to the Baptist faith under the preaching of Richard Curtis, pastor of Salem Church.[6]

But the spring thaw was still in the offing, and water in the creek was yet too chilly for a "proper baptizin' " by immersion. Determined to take full advantage of the waiting period, the Wesleyan resolved to rescue his kith and kin from a needless "dunking." Confronting Randall with Adam Clarke's doctrine of *baptizo*,[7] Tobias convinced him that "sprinkling" washed away as many sins as "going under the water," and Randall renounced his commitment to Curtis and embraced the "true faith."[8] Methodist liturgists might insert this day on their calendar of fasts and feasts.

Randall was reminded of the fact that as a barefooted lad in South Carolina he had already been "engrafted into the body of Christ's Church, and made a living member of the same."[9] Prior to the organization of the Methodist Episcopal Church in 1784-1785 the sacraments were administered to members of the Methodist Society by ordained Anglican clergy. Baptismal vows imposed a "bounden duty" upon one to share in ministry to others; to assume the responsibility for mission to "all sorts and conditions of men," whether one's white peers or his black servants. Randall could only draw one conclusion from his cousin's explanation of *baptizo*:

2

he was his brother's keeper in the world slaveholders were fashioning for themsleves and their posterity in the heartland of the Cotton Kingdom.[10] He was already immersed in "the world"—not in a warm creek.

His enthusiasm was immediately translated into his more familiar realm of "worldly" affairs. He arranged with business associates in the territorial capital to provide an appropriate preaching place for his cousin. The trustees of an old field school, which Randall's family patronized and supported, offered their facility freely.[11] In view of the widespread religious revival sweeping the frontier at that time, the arrangement was apparently not protested.[12] Moreover, "rowdies" would find the spectacle highly entertaining and profitable for their sale of Demon Rum![13]

Neither the date nor the extent of this initial revival conducted by a Methodist preacher in Mississippi is known. In terms of religious results the record is clear: eight souls, six whites and two blacks, were admitted to membership in the Methodist Society. Their names or identity deserve at least a mention in state history books: Randall and Harriet Gibson, William and Rachel Foster, Edna Bullen, Caleb Worley, and a manslave and his wife. The black couple belonged either to Randall or William, whose plantation was located at Pine Ridge above Natchez. Reflecting on this obscure moment in Mississippi history at the end of Reconstruction, John Griffing Jones exclaimed: "This was indeed a sublime spectacle!"[14]

It was especially sublime for Tobias. Before departing Charleston he had manumitted his slaves after a struggle with his conscience and possible difficulties with the law. Thirty-six years later, when the defense of the "peculiar institution" was emerging as a southern crusade, the Fosters freed twenty-one of their slaves for colonization in Liberia.[15] That the "Gibson doctrine" had all those years never been

3

erased from their thoughts is a probability which cannot be discounted. It was this visible result, rather than the mere addition of names to the church rolls, which characterized the more enduring fruits of the primitive Wesleyan revival in the Washington schoolhouse at the turn of the century.[16]

During the next three years Tobias preached his gospel and organized congregations in settlements along the river counties from Fort Adams to Walnut Hills. Masters and slaves shared the Lord's Supper at the same primitive altars. By that time, however, Gibson began to sense a sullen recalcitrancy among some of his white communicants to the practice of sharing the Bread of Life with their black chattels. The elusory feeling of alienation was reflected on the faces of both races. Then when defections among his white flock began to mount, and absences from love feasts reached epidemic proportions, he realized that his doctrine was threatened and his evangelical effectiveness was waning.[17]

Depressed and sapped of physical stamina by consumption, he rode to Kentucky seeking help from Bishop Asbury and the Western Annual Conference in 1802 and again in 1803.[18] He needed a helper, a "junior preacher." The empathetic bishop explained that he had none to send. His small band of missionaries was thinly spread over a vast territory west of the Alleghenies extending from the Great Lakes to the Gulf of Mexico. Just as Tobias was saddling up to return home alone, an adventurous circuit rider named Moses Floyd was so mesmerized by Gibson's glowing story of Natchez belles and beaus that he volunteered to ride with him to "Elysian Fields."[19]

Their dialogue during the long ride down the Trace from Sumner County must have been a gem of lost oral history. It was probably not about magnolias and hoop skirts, but about a beachhead encircled by land-hungry slave drivers—a distant Wesleyan enclave which could be secured only by the grace of God and an army of evangelical giants. A short time after this first team ministry dismounted in Mississippi, Moses succumbed to the charms of Hannah Griffing, sister of Sarah, with whom Tobias had fallen in love but never married.[20]

As atonement for Floyd's "elopement" and abrupt "location," Asbury dispatched Hezekiah Harriman and Abraham Amos to the Natchez Country. Soon afterward the former fell victim of a fever, and the latter hastened back to his native habitat in search of greener pastures. The defeated and distraught Gibson died on April 5, 1804. His South Carolina brethren praised his heroic efforts.[21] His Mississippi flock buried him in an unmarked grave dug by a young slave to whom he had probably extended the right hand of Christian fellowship. On receiving the distressing news of Tobias' demise, the bishop wondered if mission to Mississippi may have been interred with his protégé's emaciated corpse.[22]

Asbury was absent from sessions of the Western Conference at Mount Gerizim, Kentucky, in October following Gibson's death. In his stead William McKendree, presiding elder of an extensive district in the West, was elected to preside.[23] When an anti-slavery Ohio brother suggested that mission in Gibson's fated vineyard should be abandoned, McKendree refused to recognize any such motion. He sternly warned his fainthearted brother that "those little isolated Societies far down in the South" would be sustained without counting the cost. When the appointments were read during those anxious moments before adjournment, the names of three men were assigned the task of walking in Gibson's moccasins."[24]

Lerner (Learner) Blackman was an "organization man."[25] Since the days of their founder, sometimes called "Pope John,"[26] Wesleyans had prided themselves for this gift of pragmatic ability. Nathan (C. T. N.) Barnes was assigned to serve under Blackman. He was a studious, soft-spoken man with whom the collegium of Natchez intellectuals would feel much at ease.[27] McKendree announced that if the peripatetic Lorenzo Dow could be found in the hills and persuaded to repeat a previous excursion into Alabama, he would be a "natural" to capitalize on the revival stirred by Gibson. After a scout familiar with his trail finally found him, Lorenzo joined Blackman and Barnes for the November ride down the Trace.[28]

They emerged from "The Wilderness"[29] with saddlebags stuffed full of plans for outreach to the sparsely populated settlements of the country. Their first order of business was to call a quarterly meeting on Clarke's Creek,[30] but before the agenda could be completed a rip-roaring revival broke out. The unpredictable Lorenzo was simply unable to restrain his impulse to preach, but it brought forth good fruit. Backsliders who had turned on Gibson for converting as many slaves to the fold as masters were admonished to repent and return to the Wesleyan way. One elderly defector hobbled to the "pulpit stand," fell to his knees confessing his sins, and others followed "under conviction." News of the awakening and the announcement of a follow-up camp meeting to be conducted near Washington in December spread like wildfire along the bayous and through the piney woods east of Natchez.[31]

"Camp meeting" was a new word to Mississippi settlers. During revivals they could get happy, roll in the leaves and shout for an evening before returning home to a warm bed.[32] But to load up a family and gear in a wagon and go to preaching in the woods for days and nights on end during December, with little more than campfires and the preacher's fiery sermons to keep them warm, was sheer insanity. It was little wonder, then, that campers often hid their jugs in their buckboards to keep the fading embers alive. Enterpreneurs were not above hauling barrels of whiskey to nearby "places of refreshment" to fuel the fires of penitents.[33]

Skeptics of this novel idea suspected that Dow's camp meeting would end up in a drunken orgy. Andrew Marschalk, editor of the Natchez *Mississippi Herald and Gazette*, vented his sharpest satire on this wild circus-in-the-woods.[34] It was only after Lorenzo related his experiences with the Presbyterians in Kentucky and Tennessee during recent camp meetings,[35] that the dour Randall finally agreed to cosponsor the ambitious ecumenical venture. When the meeting horn was sounded, he and his family and their slaves loaded up and wound their way into the stately oak grove near the seat of territorial government.[36]

By nightfall shouts of Halleluiah! echoed in the forest. Some fifty souls were awakened, and "five professed to find peace with God."[37] As usual, Lorenzo was the star performer. But Randall Gibson, John Ellis and James Hoggatt were not overly impressed with his brand of evangelism. They were currently involved in the affairs of Jefferson College, "a fruitful Nursery of Science and Virtue,"[38] graces not necessarily synonymous with religious enthusiasm. In fact, they considered Blackman to be the more "worthy successor of the sainted Gibson." He impressed them as a man of truer Wesleyan stature—a man blessed with a head as well as a heart.[39]

By the first of the year Blackman had set himself to the ponderous task of drafting a master plan for mission beyond the immediate Natchez region. Anticipating the time when the Methodist arm would reach deeper into Louisiana and Alabama, he prepared to lay his scheme before Bishop Asbury, Richard Whatcoat,[40] and members of the Western Conference in 1805. After arriving by horseback for the Kentucky conclave in the autumn, he presented his projections to sympathetic brethren with McKendree looking over his shoulder. He pointed out that since the end of the Spanish regime the population of the region between the Choctaw line and parallel 31 degrees had increased to some 4,500 whites and 2,400 slaves, and that the increase of the total population was expected to reach 75,000 during the ensuing decade.[41] The harvest was white; laborers were few.

In a sheer act of apostolic faith, Yankee preachers, who had never blazed distant southern trails, dispatched four volunteers to ride with Blackman to "The Natchez." William Pattison, a young recruit from Ohio, was appointed to Claiborne Circuit, embracing Warren and Jefferson counties. Thomas Easley, son of a Virginia preacher, was assigned as Barnes' assistant on the Natchez Circuit. Caleb W. Cloud, an Ohioan in his first year, was sent to Wilkinson Circuit.[42] Elisha W. Bowman, a Virginian who was later called on the carpet for "wearing weapons to inspire terror," was commissioned to secure a foothold in New Orleans and explore the bayou country of eastern Louisiana.[43]

Bidding Elisha godspeed before boarding a barge at Natchez Landing, Blackman admonished him to disarm himself. This may have saved Elisha's neck. On arriving in New Orleans, Blackman was immediately embroiled in fisticuffs with a gang of rowdies from whom he escaped with no more than a black eye. After this rude introduction to the city, he sought out the more genteel company of "respectable" Episcopalians who had migrated from his native state. On finding their priest, Philander Chase,[44] he solicited his influence in securing a place to preach. As a former circuit rider himself, Philander readily responded with the suggestion that his black-eyed visitor apply for use of the Government House fronting Saint Louis Cathedral.

On the following Sunday the Methodist appeared at the Capitol only to find the doors locked. When he heard that his "Episcopalian brethren were at the bottom of all this,"[45] he was justifiably incensed. Shaking "off the dirt" from "this ungodly city," he rode off to Opelousas. There he was met by "a few Americans who were swearing with almost every breath." Barging into their midst and brandishing his Bible, he was advised that "the priest swore as hard as they did," and that he played cards and danced with them after Sunday mass. Undeterred by this blasphemous reception to bayou culture, he rode through watery wastes for a year in search of lost souls until the limbs of his horse were "skinned and rough to his hock joints." But he succeeded in rescuing seventeen wandering sheep from the bogholes of this "Romish quagmire."[46]

This tentative foothold in the bayous swelled Blackman's roll of converts during 1806 to one hundred and thirty-four whites and twenty-seven blacks, freedmen as well as slaves. Yet when he arrived for the sessions of the Western Conference at Ebenezer Church in Greene County, Kentucky, he was confronted with the identical problem which Gibson had encountered. A vocal faction of antislavery Ohioans accused him of compromising Wesleyan principles to the whims of slaveholders, and that he had done so with the tacit blessing of Asbury.[47] At that moment McKendree intervened and saved Blackman and the Mississippi mission from punitive action and a ban on further appointments to the territory.[48]

Thus Bowman was left undisturbed in his free-wheeling mission. He pressed on to the Ouachita region, where he dug in every stump hole in search of prostrate sinners. On Prairie Mer Rouge he uncovered Americans from Virginia and the Carolinas who "knew little more about the nature of salvation than untaught Indians." "I have to learn them to sing," he sighed.[49]

Back in Natchez the more "fashionable" Methodists had determined that sheaves could be gathered to the fold in a more sophisticated manner. They began building a well-appointed brick church for "Sunday preaching" with a melodeon for "choir-singing." They insisted that Tobias Gibson would best be honored by a permanent memorial to his memory.[50] Yet Cokesbury Chapel was neither named for him nor built on the muddy beachhead where he first set foot. The structure was raised by black masons on a lot fronting Fifth (Union) Street north of Main at a cost of $3,500 during 1807.[51] Local nabobs of several religious persuasions contributed to the undertaking. Here, they boasted, ecumenically minded Methodists were establishing their "cathedral" city for mission to the fringes of the Old Southwest.

In their enthusiasm for "more culture in the pulpit" they had overlooked two poignant realities. First, Gibson's grave was gathering bramble. Second, the price which Blackman and his men had paid to build up the walls of Zion in this land of "wild beasts and heathen people" was incalculable. The penniless leader and his five itinerants rode away from "The Natchez" for the last time, leaving planters to enjoy their comfortable pews, and the polyglot populace of New Orleans to praise the Devil.[52]

Antislavery Ohioans gloated over this stroke of divine retribution meted out to a gainsaying people. When they gathered for the Western Conference at Chillicothe in 1807 they were armed with their *onus probandi*. They pointed out that since Gibson's day only one soul had been converted to the Wesleyan fold in any given week. Virtually blackmailing the tottering Asbury, they presented him with a mandate: either leave Natchez to the same fate as New Orleans, or appoint an antislavery man to the post vacated by Blackman. Their strategy was successful. David Young, a veteran noted for his "pertinence of speech," was appointed presiding elder of the Mississippi District.[53]

Young's men had already been handpicked in a party caucus: James Axley, Richard Browning, Anthony Houston, Jedidiah McMinn and John Travis. Each possessed "fascinating gifts" capable of exciting "the public mind"—gifts which at the end of 1808 were to prove their undoing. When called to give an account of their evangelical stewardship, the cold figures revealed a "marked decrease" in white membership. In Cokesbury Chapel alone, the number of white communicants had dwindled from one hundred and seventeen to sixty-five.[54] Young and his preachers had simply spoken too many unsavory words out of season. His aversion to slavery was to surface resoundingly during the debates which tore American Methodism apart thirty-six years afterward.[55]

Mississippians were possibly spared a localized form of this shipwreck at an earlier date by the election of McKendree to the episcopacy in 1808. Although the intellectual Easterner, Nathan Bangs, branded him "an awkward backwoodsman," Mississippians called him a Wesleyan giant in the land.[56] Deeply disturbed by reversals among distant brethren he had never seen, the new bishop summarily recalled Axley, Browning, Travis and Young from their posts.

His aggressive use of episcopal authority backfired on him. His handpicked appointees, led by John McClure, a "good weak man" co-opted for his "toadyism," proved unequal to their tasks. They, too, were recalled at the end of one year. A foreboding miasma seemed to haunt their mission, and Randall Gibson, William Foster and other laypersons began to wonder if their land was being exploited by an absentee hierarchy bent on manumitting their slaves and serving as a dumping ground for clerical castoffs incapable of ministering to their famishing souls. The bishop's intentions were open to question.[57]

But they misjudged McKendree. In 1809 he sent to Natchez nine of the strongest traveling preachers in the Western Conference, replete with marching orders to strengthen the stakes and lengthen the cords of mission under the watchful eye of Miles Harper. When the conference convened in Shelbyville, Kentucky, one year later, Asbury and McKendree led in the singing of a *Te Deum* praising the Lord for the passing of two years of "stagnation" in Gibson Country. With the cession of remaining Spanish territories to the United States in that same year, the bishops prepared their meager forces to move in and possess the land.[58]

Their only problem—one that was common to every organized body of evangelicals on the frontier—was one of adequate manpower. Eighty rawboned men on horseback could hardly be expected to cover such a vast area of mid-America with the good news of scriptural holiness. Men of lesser moral stature would probably have despaired of their mission. William Mitchell might not have volunteered for a solitary venture into upper Ohio and the whole of the Michigan peninsula.[59] Sela Paine and William Winans might have turned deaf ears to pleas for volunteers to augment Harper's thin line of weary saddlemen in the "dreaded Natchez."[60]

If Harper was not an autocrat, he was surely a maverick. While riding with his men down the Trace he discarded the orders of the bishops in the wayside bushes. He placed his workers where men and mission fitted together. He was immune to hurt feelings. Like Moses, he kept one eye on his restless flock and the other on the Promised Land. No myopia clouded his vision of total mission to the uttermost reaches of the southern frontier. To the south and west of Natchez an enchanting expanse of bayouland loomed before his eager eyes. To the southeast the crystalline beaches and tranquil bays of the Gulf Country stretched from New Orleans to Pensacola. To the east and north of Natchez, reaching across the Tombigbee, lay a piney woods paradise through which red men roamed at will.[61]

In his impetuous way Lorenzo Dow had shared the same vision. Prior to Gibson's death he had appeared out of nowhere at "a considerable settlement" on the Tensas River inhabited by pioneers of English descent from Georgia and the Carolinas. In the wake of his excursion his converts appealed to the South Carolina Conference to send them a preacher. The old Western Conference was apparently overloaded with Ohioans! Responding to their request, Gibson's old conference sent Matthew P. Sturdevant to "Tombecbee" in 1807. In the meantime, scattered "camp fires" were being kindled by river travelers on the upper Tombigbee, the Alabama and the Black Warrior.[62]

Bishop McKendree placed these missions under the control of the Natchez-based preachers. Mobile or Montgomery would have been the more obvious command posts for these settlements, but the bishop apparently thought otherwise. For one thing, like New Orleans, Catholic Mobile was suspect. For another, he was convinced that the most likely axis for mission astride the Mississippi would be Natchez.[63] Finally, he concluded that Mississippi would be the first to organize an autonomous annual conference in the foreseeable future. All of this he made clear to Harper in 1809.

It is also possible that the western-born bishop may have been romantically drawn to the fabled lifestyle of Natchez culture. His partiality for "Southern Life" by the riverside where Gibson left his indelible moccasin mark is evident from his later visits to hospitable homes in Adams and Wilkinson counties. Moreover, during conference at Shelbyville he realized that the "greatest increase in membership" was not in Mobile or New Orleans, but "on the Natchez and Wilkinson Circuits" adjacent to Feliciana, Saint Helena and Washington parishes below parallel 31 degrees in Louisiana. For these reasons he co-opted a "small but strong corps" of saddlemen: John Henninger, William Houston, John Jennings, Thomas Nelson, Sela Paine, Isaac Quinn, Samuel Sellers, Hezekiah Shaw, Frederick D. Wimberly and William Winans. In addition, South Carolina sent John S. Ford and John W. Kennon to the Alabama missions.[64]

Unlike their romance smitten predecessor, Moses Floyd, these men knew where harness buckles chafed most painfully. And they were Wesleyan realists. None was hoodwinked into thinking that he would be sipping afternoon tea with nabobs on spacious verandas of Natchez mansions. None expected to be greeting hoop-skirted belles after "Sunday Church." None dreamed of lazy cruises aboard river packets down to New Orleans for Mardi Gras.[65] There was yet no "Rosalie," no "Stanton Hall."[66] The steamer *New Orleans* had not yet been built.[67]

They were "the sent" to a world of endless bayous and forbidding forests, a cruel and unforgiving world of savagery and beauty, moccasins and May flowers, balmy eventides "reeking with pestilence" and the sweet fragrance of honeysuckle. During a "protracted meeting" Harper assured his men that in this land of strange contrasts and inordinate passions they would share love feasts with staunch souls of pristine faith in God and crippling superstitions of natural phenomena in His created world.[68]

In a brief time nature confirmed Harper's words. During 1811 a wave of massive earthquakes reaching from Missouri to New Orleans altered the course of the Mighty Mississippi and left a residue of devastation in its wake.[69] One sadistic entrepreneur capitalized on the effects of the catastrophe by putting out a broadside predicting that a great comet would collide with the earth near Natchez at one o'clock on October 24. On the eve of doomsday Randall Gibson huddled with his family and their pastor for a final prayer meeting on earth.[70] Praying with tongue in cheek, the preacher was sufficiently versed in natural astronomy to realize that by morning the heavenly visitor would be on the opposite side of the earth. "What an awful jolt we should have!" reads his diary.[71]

Earthquakes, fires, floods and wayward comets were simply God's way of jolting sinners to repentance. Within months a potential catastrophe of man's making appeared on the horizon: "Madison's War" with Great Britain.[72] It could easily spell the death knell for Methodism in Mississippi, Alabama and Louisiana. It could isolate her from Mother Church and leave her a helpless orphan to perish by the riverside. This ominous possibility was made painfully clear to Harper and his flock as events of 1812-1813 slowly surfaced following the declaration of war on June 18, 1812.[73]

In 1812 the General Conference, the supreme legislative body of the church, disbanded the Western Annual Conference and placed the Mississippi District under the new Tennessee Conference.[74] At the same time the Natchez-based preachers were authorized to organize their own annual conference pending the presence of a bishop. Asbury and McKendree were present for formalities at Reese's Chapel, Tennessee, October 1, 1813, but they were warned not to venture into Mississippi through hostile Indian territory. Frontier bishops may have been valorous, but they were not anxious to sacrifice their scalps. For the same reason, Samuel Dunwoody, who was supposed to come from South Carolina as Harper's successor, never arrived at Natchez.[75]

One month prior to the Tennessee conclave the garrison and civilians of Fort Mims had been massacred by the Creek Indians.[76] Shortly before that infamous day word spread that six hundred Creeks were approaching Grindstone Ford on the Trace to link up with other marauding tribes or Redcoat spies at Natchez.[77] Entire neighborhoods fled into the woods, in one instance led by a circuit rider armed to the teeth. Before locking the doors of his store, one tightfisted merchant gave away shot and black powder indiscriminately.[78]

During the epidemic of consternation the preachers were able to gather an unprecedented number of souls into the Methodist fold—a total of eight hundred and nine—raising the district membership to 1,641 whites and 475 blacks. War hysteria was no deterrent to the determination of Mississippians to structure their own annual conference, now that a grand total of over two thousand communicants had been attained. The threatened orphan was prepared to stand on her two feet. Any retreat was unthinkable. Tobias Gibson had secured the beachhead; they were commissioned to break out into the hostile hinterland.[79]

On November 1, 1813, twelve disciples of John Wesley rode to Newit Vick's place five miles southwest of Fayette to organize the Mississippi Annual Conference. Their host, an "aristocratic" Virginian and local preacher, was prevented by church law from direct participation in the proceedings. Only traveling preachers were accorded seats in a conference. Nonetheless, his counsel was apparently sought by the less sophisticated itinerants who were impatient with jots and tittles of official directives from absentee bureaucrats. Like Thomas Owens, who had previously served the Devil with a passion, they meant to get on with the Lord's business. This they proceeded to do with the full exercise of their "indomitable moral nature."[80]

With only $202.18 in their common treasury, and having no bishop present to ordain men on trial or deacons ready for elder's orders, they formed a quasi-conference before bidding the Vicks adieu. They elected Samuel Sellers as their presiding elder. High on his agenda of priorities was the assault on New Orleans, the southern "emporium of sin." It mattered little to him that the armada of the Crown lurked in the offshore waters. Wesleyan pride demanded that he justify the aborted effort of Elisha Bowman by sending young William Winans to the port city two weeks after adjournment at Vick's. At the landing where Gibson had beached his canoe, Sellers armed his deacon with thirty dollars to buy books from the Methodist Book Concern in New

York. Books and tracts were indispensable evangelical weapons against sin in high places.[81]

By this time the war had moved ever closer to Mississippi soil. Although Andrew Jackson and his Tennessee Volunteers had recently encamped northeast of Natchez, and Thomas Hinds had conducted his "Indian Hunt" on Lower Peach Tree prior to the massacre at Fort Mims, the Creeks were still on the warpath. It was not until the Battle of Horseshoe Bend in April of 1814 that Jackson was able to subdue the Alabama tribe. Yet by that time the threat of a British invasion was spreading "excitement and turmoil" across the country.[82]

In the midst of this uncertainty the preachers convened at John Ford's Marion County home in November 1814. Only one hundred and eighty-seven souls had been added to the rolls during the year, and losses among the blacks numbered thirty-five. The reports could hardly have been otherwise. The call to arms had reduced the size of congregations to "little more than a moiety of what, in other circumstances, they would have been." The usual comforts of life were denied to master and slave alike. Coffee drinkers on the plantations were compelled to brew their morning pick-up from okra seed on awaking to the sad fact that they had fallen on hard times together.[83]

An uncommonly severe winter compounded the misery of the season of leanness. Inflammatory symptoms were pandemic. Slaves collapsed in the fields. Mortality among whites in the river counties reached unprecedented heights. Virtually every preacher leaving Ford's was on the verge of stumbling headlong into some muddy slough. Making his way to Attakapas, the ascetical Richmond Nolley fell from his saddle, rested his head on a pine knot, and quietly expired during the freezing night of November 25, 1814. He was buried by hunters in an unmarked grave somewhere across the river from Natchez in Catahoula Parish.[84].

On that same night, perhaps within earshot of the bog where this giant of a man from South Carolina had laid his weary head to sleep, lads from Adams and Jefferson counties were trudging down the Natchez-to-Baton-Rouge Road.[85] Nolley died with his dog-eared Bible in hand. Perhaps some of them were destined to die in other bogs firmly clutching a different kind of a weapon. One was a soldier in the Wesleyan ranks; the others were recruits in Old Hickory's command.[86]

Within two short months following the eyeball-to-eyeball encounter with Redcoats in the marshes below New Orleans, survivors would be retracing their steps along this same river road toward the barren fields and hills of home. Few were the shouts of victory along the line of march. Knapsacks which once bulged with ill-fitting articles of general issue and intimate mementos of loved ones were now empty of all save nightmares of a firefight across the breastworks of a cypress ditch.

Although casualties in the ranks of the Jefferson Troop and other units of Mississippi militia were minimal, many fell victim of diseases induced by exposure to the chilling dampness of a winter campaign. Circuit riders made their weary way from one family burial plot to another, pausing only long enough to offer comforting words to the bereaved. For them the river road was no longer a winding path bordered by endless rows of fragrant flowers of which romantic novelists wrote so glowingly in afteryears. In their diaries the veteran preachers could only write of a trail of tears.[87] But they learned some lasting lessons from this impulse of a new Republic "to pull John Bull by the nose."[88]

They remembered and taught their people to remember that it was not white men alone who manned that boggy breach below New Orleans on a cold January day in 1815. Crouched shoulder-to-shoulder beside them in the slimy cypress ditch, and standing at-the-ready in reserve, were free black men from Louisiana and scores of Choctaw and Chickasaw braves from the virgin forests of Mississippi and Alabama.[89] On the field of battle in defense of their fatherland, no man's blood spilled upon the mud seemed to differ from another man's. Nor were their petitions to the Almighty, uttered in dialects and tongues foreign to another's ear, indiscernible to another's heart. Lerner Blackman, chaplain of Jackson's brigade, was never more convinced of the truth that God was "no respecter of persons" than in this brief encounter with Edward Pakenham's combat veterans.[90]

Perhaps the more "worldly" lesson which Blackman's fellow-Methodists learned from this eventful moment in American history was best put by one of his unlettered colleagues. William Winans was compelled to confess that those "cherished tendencies to coldness and alienation," so common to established communities and cultures "in times of peace and prosperity," were virtually obliterated when souls were "tried in the fire." Calamity, or even the threat of it, he cautiously concluded, may well have been as efficacious as divine grace in reconciling the races of humankind each to the other, and of "exciting mutual sympathy" between them.[91] While penning these thoughts on the eve of the War between the States, the tottering circuit rider wondered if Gibson's beachhead could withstand the assault forces arrayed against it from within and without.

Two: Breakout to the Bayous and Piney Woods

The Methodists are inseparably intertwined with the history of this state . . . The pioneer circuit rider provided the inspiration for succeeding generations.

Paul B. Johnson, Jr.

The Methodists were not the first evangelical Protestants to campaign for the soul of Mississippi. They were, however, the first to organize their forces as a formal ecclesiastical body for mission to settlers in the piney woods and along the bayous of the Mississippi Territory.[1] Their organizing conference, which convened at the home of Newit Vick in November of 1813, anteceded the formation of the Presbytery of Mississippi by three years, the Episcopal Diocese of Mississippi by thirteen years, and the State Baptist Convention by twenty years. Formal organization of the Lutheran Synod of Mississippi was yet forty-two years in the future, and it was not until 1844 that the Disciples of Christ created their state association.[2]

In the antebellum era Episcopal Methodism was a clerically dominated ecclesiology or form of church government. She operated her "system" strictly by disciplinary "Rule." Both the General Conference and annual (territorial) conferences were composed of bishops (general superintendents) and itinerant preachers exclusively. Laypersons and persons licensed to preach (local preachers) were excluded from seat, voice, vote and direct participation in conference proceedings. In a word, total authority in matters of faith and morals was vested in ordained members of the itinerant ministry.

The gathering at Vick's apparently included several local preachers and laypersons. Randall Gibson and William Foster were probably present and, true to their practical nature, cautioned the enthusiastic preachers against premature decisions and actions which in the long run might prove to be counterproductive for "efficient" mission. Others questioned the legality of creating an annual conference in the absence of a bishop. Yet basking still in the afterglow of the Revolution, a majority was so imbued with the spirit of independence and expansionist missionary zeal as to rule the day. It is not unlikely that the squabbling brethren were reminded by their host that his fellow-Virginian, Thomas Jefferson, had also been confronted by skeptics who doubted the wisdom of his landmark declaration drafted in 1776.[3]

Even so, the cautionary words of Gibson, a local preacher, Foster, a layman, and Winans, an itinerant, were not without rational merit. First, they could have pointed out that American Methodism herself, being less than thirty years of age, had not yet fully coordinated her farflung forces for concerted mission to the frontier.[4] Second, since no bishop was present to ordain elders, an essential sacerdotal element necessary to a total ministry of word and sacrament was missing. No clerical candidate or deacon among them was permitted by the *Ordinal* to feed his famished sheep with the Bread of Life and Wine of the Soul at the Lord's Table.[5] The scattered flock must be content to survive on crumbs and branch water.

At that moment in history the Mississippi Methodists were like a lonely pine needle lazily drifting by in the placid waters of Bayou Pierre. Solitary "junior preachers" were destined to drift for three years before an episcopal father would sign their foreheads with the Mark of Melchizedek. During that anxious interim the tenuous structure of the conference and the morale of her men were to suffer grievously. Defections among the preachers and their constituents became epidemic. More than one in every two traveling preachers either retired to his farm or former trade, or simply made for the Trace to ride north in search of that elusive lea hidden in the romantic heart of every Wesleyan itinerant.[6]

When the preachers gathered for conference at Adams Campground in the autumn of 1815—sometimes called "the lost conference"—more than one-half of her "effective force" was missing.[7] Nolley was dead. Jonathan Kemp, Roswell Valentine and Gabriel Pickering had stepped down from the ranks and were "discontinued." John S. Ford and Thomas A. King had sought asylum in Tennessee. John I. E. Byrd had married Margaret, the sister of future Governor John Jones McRae, and "located."[8] William Winans had also located after his marriage to Martha Nettles Dubose (DuBose) of "Elysian Fields" in western Amite and eastern Wilkinson counties.[9]

Only four traveling preachers remained on Samuel Sellers' appointment list for 1816, marking the lowest manpower point in over a decade.[10] Distressed by this intolerable attrition in the ranks, Bishop McKendree acted promptly and firmly. He peremptorily plucked James Dixon, Alexander Fleming, John Menefee and Thomas Nixon from the Tennessee flock, Ashley Hewitt and John Lane from South Carolina, and dispatched them posthaste to Mississippi. Yet even this new supply of men still left several strategic missions vacant. New Orleans was left without a shepherd to bask in her "fashionable" lifestyle. Ouachita went wanting for pastoral care. The campaign so enthusiastically planned for mission to the people of the forest and dwellers along the bayous had apparently stalled in its muddy tracks.[11]

The infant conference was demoralized. All too long she had "languished in colonial dependence" upon a distant hierarchy for oversight and support. On October 10, 1816, a thin gray line of heavyhearted men rode in to William Foster's Pine Ridge plantation for what some feared would be their final session as an organized body.

During the past year at least one hundred and seventy-five white and one hundred black souls had been written off the circuit records. The sense of loss was deepened further when news of Bishop Asbury's death on March twenty-first reached the country, casting a funereal pall over the land.[12] Two months later the weight of gloom was partially alleviated by the announcement that the General Conference of 1816 had elected two bishops to assist the overworked McKendree: Robert Richford Roberts and Enoch George.[13]

Shortly after the Baltimore conclave adjourned late in the spring, reliable word reached Sellers that one of the new bishops intended to visit Mississippi in the fall. The Doubting Thomases had a field day. Promises had been broken before. Mother Church was gently but surely weaning her southern offspring for abandonment. The first day at Foster's place resembled a slighted child awaiting Santa in vain. An occluded sky greeted the sun on the following morning, refusing to dissipate until high noon.

Then at the stroke of twelve the sun, awesome in autumnal warmth and majesty, broke through the shroud of gloom. At that moment a manslave, whom Tobias may have received into the fellowship of Christ's religion sixteen years before, appeared at the door of the conference room and whispered something in the secretary's ear. Turning to his brethren, Winans announced: "Bishop Roberts has arrived!" "Little Tommy" Owens shouted as though the promise of the Second Coming had finally been fulfilled. Every voice joined in the anthem to the Year of Jubilee, echoing through the stately pines of the ridge and winging its way like a mourning dove down the winding bayous and across the fields of cotton white unto the harvest.[14]

Following a feast on turkey, venison and hickory-cured ham around Rachel's bountiful board, the "Frontier Bishop" called the first *"proper"* annual conference in the territory to order. "Present, ready and able" to bend to the task! answered the men when their names were called from the roll.

The report of the treasurer revealed a modest $499.06¼ frugally garnered for the gathering. With arrearages of only $399.06¼ due the preachers for "quarterage," the balance was evenly divided between Tennessee and Missouri for missionary outreach.[15] This poignant expression for apostolic zeal may well have been a thank offering for the, self-sacrificing labors of Tobias Gibson and Richmond Nolley. "Benevolences" over and above the biblical tithe has been the benchmark of Mississippi Methodists since earliest days.[16]

Motivated by that same spirit of charity, William Montgomery offered his Pine Ridge Presbyterian Church for the ordination service marking the climax of the conference.[17] But when the "fashionable" sanctuary proved inadequate to accomodate the crowd which gathered for the sacred rites, the bishop led them out to a stand of "spreading, umbrageous trees" where he preached from Jeremiah 9:23-24 and ordained three deacons and five presbyters (elders). "Love, justice, and righteousness in the earth," he reminded his hearers, was to be the burden of their witness to the people of the forests, fields, bayous—white men, red men, black men—populating a frontier enclave awaiting birth as a sovereign state in the Union of States eight months afterward.[18]

Little did he then suspect that this commonwealth would soon be fashioned in a frontier Methodist meeting house. Yet on July 7, 1817, the first Constitution of the State of Mississippi was signed on the rough-cut pulpit of the old Washington Church.[19]

It is an irony of state history that in the very act of affixing their signatures to that document, delegates to the convention proscribed ministers of the Gospel from holding public office. Jeremiah would have wept at the enigmatic affront to all that was holy. Incensed by this intolerable violation of natural and civil rights, religious forces of the new commonwealth joined in a moral crusade to challenge the discriminatory provision. In a short time this first ecumenical resistance movement in behalf of love, justice and righteousness reversed the direction of this early misadventure in matters political.[20]

Leading the van of forces that turned the tide of a witless venture by Mississippi politicians, the Methodists assumed the stance of a river-boat gambler. Their firm stand on the issue would either drive their constituents from their altars or attract a growing population to their church doors. The latter result proved to be the case. Three years after the Constitutional Convention adjourned, the Methodist roll of members, black as well as white, had more than doubled in numbers.[21]

A properly ordained corps of clergy and an increased constituency provided resources for an expanded campaign of mission. At the end of 1820 Tobias Gibson's original circuit had grown to four large districts in Mississippi and Louisiana and two in Alabama. In addition, the number of traveling preachers had increased to thirty, and new missions had been opened on plantations and in the Choctaw Nation.[22]

The New Orleans mission was another story. An eloquent but impatient local preacher named Mark Moore had invoked tongues of fire upon "Sin City" and collected a sizeable congregation in a rented flour loft. He then announced that the time was ripe for launching an ambitious building program. Clutching their proverbial purses, his "lay popes" rebelled. The donnybrook that ensued split the congregation down the middle, threatening the struggling enterprise with disaster. After adjourning conference at Washington in 1819, McKendree and

Winans caught a steamer at Bayou Sara and headed for the battlefield.[23]

They were met with such formidable forces that not even the seasoned frontier bishop, who read men more astutely than books,[24] was able to calm the strife. But unlike some of his brethren during the Washington sessions he was resolved that the port city would not be severed from Mother Church. With the wiliness inherent in his breed he co-opted a non-resident committee of two trusted laymen, Edward McGehee and John G. Richardson, and the preacher he would presently appoint presiding elder, Winans, to assume control of the situation. At the next conference in Midway Church during November 1820 the absentee managers recommended that Moore's loft be allowed to gather cobwebs for a year in order for tempers to cool and a new start for the soul of the city be initiated.[25]

In the meantime a new venture was being initiated within earshot of the cradle of the commonwealth. The preachers, virtually void of formal academic credentials but strongly influenced by the presence of nearby Jefferson College across the way from the Washington Church, had resolved to launch a school for young ladies. Mostly bachelors, they believed the adage about hands that rocked the cradle. Thus in 1818, assured of financial backing by laypersons including prominent state politicians, they incorporated and organized The Elizabeth Female Academy in the town of Washington.[26]

A majority of those involved in the enterprise were converts of the circuit riders. Yet the school was neither named for a Wesleyan saint nor staffed by Methodists. It bore the maiden name of the donor of land and buildings: Elizabeth Greenfield Roach, sometime Methodist, lifelong Quaker. The first president, Chilion F. Stiles, was a committed disciple of Freemasonry. Jane Sanderson, the governess, was a blue-stocking Presbyterian, but despite this "impediment" she gave "entire satisfaction" to her Methodist employers and patrons.[27]

During the second full fall semester in 1821-1822 she entertained at a formal tea. While teachers, parents, patrons, trustees, and possibly cadets from nearby Jefferson College were engaged in polite conversation, the chairman of the board was making his way through the piney woods to the home of John Jones McRae on the Chickasawhay. Giggling girls at the academy would have made great sport of their presiding elder's embarrassing nights spent sleeping in one-room cabins next to ladies. But such was the primitive character of pioneer life in the forests east of "fashionable" Natchez and Washington.[28]

The domestic indignities of pioneer life could not preempt "Sacramental Meetings" which the chairman of the board conducted en route. At Ebenezer Meeting House some one hundred penitents crowded around the altar with "deep and solemn feeling." About twenty-five whites and fifty blacks were converted. The night was spent in prayer and singing praises to the Lord for newborn souls. On reaching McRae's settlement the elder and his preachers were inundated with queries about the outside world, and before enjoying pit barbecue they were treated to a river run on Captain McRae's new steamboat.[29]

Except for one item of gossip, the conference might have been equally pleasant. It was rumored that Bishop George, "thinking more highly of himself" than he should, had deliberately reneged on his scheduled visit to the isolated settlement. Or, possibly, he decided against exposing himself to hard-bitten preachers whom he advised to cease missionary efforts on Attakapas, Rapides, and Ouachita circuits at the end of the year.[30] The "aristocratic" Virginia-born bishop apparently failed to realize that the word "retreat" had been expurgated from the saddlebag lexicons of his rawboned Mississippi circuit riders.

Their rejoinder to the bishop's alleged slight and mandate was firm and uncompromising. They pointed out the fact that their campaign for souls in the forests and along the bayous stretching from the Chickasawhay to the Red River had increased the rolls to near seven thousand whites and over thirteen hundred blacks. Indeed, during the past year the increase among the latter exceeded that of the former. Blacks at Natchez, Pine Ridge, Kingston, Washington and Ebenezer excelled in enthusiasm and gifts of the spirit.[31] Moreover, in the absence of the bishop the business sessions at McRae's were conducted "harmoniously and expeditiously."

In an action teetering on the edge of insubordination, the preachers countermanded the bishop's order to withdraw from western Louisiana missions. They voted to send Ebenezer Hearn to the Ouachita Country unaccompanied by his bride of one week. George would have been hard put to intervene in such a selfless show of evangelical zeal. Finally, the presiding elder was instructed to inform his absent overseer that a Conference Missionary Society had been created as auxiliary to the churchwide society recently authorized by the General Conference.[32] Rebellion against Mother Church was furtherest from the minds of Mississippi circuit riders.

Thirty-five men were sent to their farflung posts from the Chickasawhay council. Zealous but unschooled, most of them had been called "out from the various occupations" of rough-and-ready life. After their names had been called to serve in some godforsaken corner of the land they had come to call "Podunk," the presiding elder challenged them to "go forward" in the face of seemingly insuperable odds. He closed with the assurance that the Redeemer, who would ride with them until nations and states were "subdued unto thy sacred way," had promised to "help with few as well as many" and "bring strength out of weakness."[33]

Their weakness of the flesh—their feet of clay—

was all too often unbearably flagrant. During the year two local and four traveling preachers were either called on the carpet and sternly admonished for unbecoming conduct, or expelled for grave moral causes. One man was censored for "criminal familiarity with women, in no case extending to actual fornication." A prominent physician and local preacher was deposed for eloping with a servant girl and abandoning his family.[34]

Yet relatively few actually "fell from grace," managing somehow to cling to "the Rock of Ages." Like the steadfast remnant of their apostolic fathers, they persevered in mission. The ailing and "worldly" Ashley Hewitt assumed the heavy responsibility of "Conference Missionary" to supervise an ambitious program of outreach to slaves on the plantations and Choctaws of the forests. For the first five months of 1823 his efforts were stymied by natural forces reminiscent of the days of Noah. His missionaries spent more time fording flooded streams than in preaching the Gospel. Then in the spring an epidemic of yellow fever inflicted the *coup de grace*.[35]

By Christmas Day 1823 the waters had receded and the fever had spent its deadly force. John W. Kennon and others were counted among its many victims who were memorialized during conference at Natchez over the holidays. Arriving late, Bishop Roberts expected to find a group of somber men lamenting their grievous losses. As he dismounted he heard the voices of singing men in the anteroom. Opening the door, he was greeted with a Yuletide gift—an illuminated map of "Operation '24." Tommy Owens had apparently addressed it to "Yankee Doubters, General Conference, Baltimore, 1824."[36]

The time had come for Mississippi preachers to enlighten the Eastern Establishment, to speak out boldly in the supreme council of the church. For a quarter of a century Mississippi had struggled against a mountain of odds, virtually ignored by her Yankee brethren, her land and her people not infrequently scored by carping critics. Now for the first time she was resolved to lay her case in a graphic fashion before the whole church. The bishop not only lauded Hewitt and his helpers for creating their masterplan for mission, but also for the "Methodistical" manner by which it was to be administered.[37]

The Natchez conference elected three delegates to the upcoming General Conference, assigned Henry P. Cook to the Mobile-Pensacola area, Wiley Ledbetter to the Choctaw Nation, and several men to plantation missions. Winans was elected "Agent for building a Church" in New Orleans, and in an artless caucus nominated as vice-president of the churchwide Missionary Society.[38] With the bishop's blessing, "Operation '24" was set in motion by forty-six men who rode away from Natchez as the New Year dawned.

Two weeks later the bishop, Daniel DeVinne, Alexander Sale and Winans mounted up and made for the Trace. Winding their way through the stately forests they gradually envisioned the primitive domain of the Choctaw and Chickasaw as a civilized Christian paradise where children could build little tepees touching the tips of graceful pines against a cloudless sky. But pragmatic Methodist men were not deceived by specious dreams.[39]

They suspected that their plan for mission might be lost in the bitter controversy currently raging across their church between Reformers, bent on diluting the authority of the bishops, and Constitutionalists, who clung to the principles of primitive Wesleyan faith and order. Easterners were virtually unanimous in their support of the reform movement with which antislavery leaders in New England were intimately associated. Southerners were equally determined to maintain "the old order of things" and allow no abolitionist pressure to curtail their mission to the slaves. At times it appeared that the Baltimore sessions would be paralyzed by sectional infighting between eastern "liberals" and southern "conservatives."[40]

Two New England "conservatives," Elijah Hedding and Joshua Soule, were elected bishops.[41] No southern candidate was considered. In Yankee eyes, for the most part, he would have epitomized all that was evil in slavery. Yet it was the Mississippi delegation which openly lobbied for the New Englanders.[42] As a reward for this support Bostonians moved to proscribe slaveholders from any office in the church, and Reformers seconded their motion. Soule was so infuriated by the tactics of the "liberal" coalition that he refused to be consecrated until each annual conference was permitted, "where state laws" allowed slavery, to shape her own rules on the subject. After this, DeVinne refused to return to Mississippi.[43]

While great issues of polity and slavery were being debated in Baltimore, Hewitt was busy doing his homework. He had received word from Winans that doors had been opened by Bishop Roberts on the ride to Baltimore through Choctaw country. The bishop and his men had breakfasted with Chieftain Greenwood LeFlore and received his approval for Ledbetter's efforts in the Nation. But the impulsive missionary had not yet learned to decipher the fine print of the Choctaw dialect.[44] Contrary to Roberts' instruction he opened a school for native children on borrowed money, went dangerously into debt, and exposed himself to the mercies of a scalping party.[45]

Roberts was forewarned of the *faux pas* prior to his coming to conference late in 1825. The Choctaw mission was "at an end;" the grand plan was virtually dead, wrote Winans. Six months later both Soule and Roberts rode into Washington like knights in full armor galloping into the fray. They informed their saddlemen that the campaign for souls in the forests would not be summarily abandoned. Somewhere out there in a hidden corner of this vast land, they insisted, a giant of a man waited to be anointed to speak comfortably to a Bedouin people, to bind up their wounds, and to embrace them as brothers in Christ.[46]

The prophet Samuel found Saul in the hayfield. Hewitt, Winans and Thomas Griffin found their man in the canebrake—a traveling preacher and physician named Alexander Talley, who had renounced a life of ease and lucrative practice in nabob circles for the poverty of circuit life. Moreover, he was strongly tainted with "liberal" reform principles and antislavery sentiments. He believed in offering "the waters of life to all," and felt called to "gather the outcasts" into "the fold of the benevolent shepherd." Within two years he was to pack his gear and apothecary in his saddlebags and ride off into "the almost unbroken forests" of the Choctaw Nation.[47]

Talley's mission to red men was as short-lived as it was stellar. In the fall of 1828 white men rode to their polling places and elevated a man to the White House who had vowed to drive the red man into exile and seize his sacred domain for the benefit of "civilized" men. And this, Andrew Jackson resolved to do in the name of *"Liberty."*[48]

It is an obscure irony of American history that on Christmas Day following the election a small band of frontier preachers gathered for conference in Tuscaloosa and dared to defy Old Hickory's Indian Policy.[49] They converted the Nativity Story into the Choctaw Story. Talley acted as narrator for the dramatic skit. LeFlore's emissary, Captain Washington, served as commentator in his native tongue. A group of young natives composed the cast. Reflective circuit riders and spectators wondered if the angelic choir of Bethlehem and the tongues of fire at Pentecost had not joined in celebrating this festive moment in eternity.[50]

The captain was immersed in his account of awakenings during a camp meeting deep in the forest. The chief and his family had all been "bathed in tears as if they were completely subdued to the gospel of Christ." Captain Offa Homa ("Red Dog") confessed that he seemed to have "two hearts:" one "little, weak heart" which made him happy; one "savage heart" which drove him to shed a brother's blood and drink his whiskey. William LeFlore's "noble-looking" wife wept as though her heart was "utterly dissolved in penitential sorrow." Closing his dramatic description of forest people caught up in the spirit of the Lord, "Red Dog" described how he had sighted "a little bright light like a candle" glowing beyond his arm's length, and he "commenced pushing though the bushes and briers" in his struggle to touch it.[51]

Overwhelmed with ecstasy, Bishop Soule arose and exclaimed: "Brethren, the Choctaw Nation is our's! No! I mistake! The Choctaw Nation is Jesus Christ's!"[52]

Joshua Soule was neither a Democrat nor a fool. He was an astute Wesleyan political tactician; and he understood the diabolical designs of demagogues who latched onto high-sounding terms like "liberty" and "freedom" to shape the affairs of the Choctaw and determine his destiny. He suspected that before Jacksonian Democracy had finally run its course the red man would be subjected to a form of slavery far worse than that in which the black man was trapped. The hunter would become the hunted; his dearest natural and civil rights would be irreparably violated.[53]

Shortly after the presidential election Governor Gerald C. Brandon urged the General Assembly of Mississippi to adopt Jackson's Indian Policy.[54] Complying with his recommendation, the legislature enacted a bill designed to remove the people of the forest to the West, beginning with the Chickasaw. One year later the Choctaw was subjected to the same statute.[55] Undaunted by this ugly political gauntlet thrown upon their wilderness trail, Talley, Robert D. Smith and Moses Perry pushed deeper into the piney woods. By the time the final bell tolled its requiem for the first citizens of the state at Dancing Rabbit Creek, two hundred and forty-three red men, women and children had been embraced by their Methodist brethren in that one year alone.[56]

In his zeal to convert the red man to his religious faith, the white man had contributed to his dark destiny. For the Methodist preacher the moral dilemma was maddening. He feared he had rescued a child from certain death only to pierce its heart with a sword. Not a few evangelists sought to resolve their quandary by sublimating their high moral principles to the demands of expediency. The objects of their fervent missionary campaign, they reluctantly concluded, were never to become "an integral part" of the white man's society—never to enjoy the fruits of his "laborious civilization."[57]

Having aborted a major campaign for the soul of the forest people, the Methodists went about their business of fortifying conference machinery for advances on other fronts. Benjamin Michael Drake assumed command of the beleaguered New Orleans mission. He secured an option on a lot in the heart of the English-speaking community and raised some $3,000 to build a sanctuary. A large share of the credit for this turnabout from what might have been a flour-loft conflagration was due to a revival conducted by William M. Curtiss, local preacher turned businessman, and Woodville industrialist Edward McGehee.[58] The "dyspeptic" McKendree must have smiled at the thought that laypersons could accomplish miracles denied his impetuous preachers.

Moreover, encouraging reports of mission in western Louisiana and the Mobile-Pensacola area appeared on the conference journal for several successive years after 1825. One year later a Holy Ghost revival broke out in the Female Academy. A cloudburst of The Spirit "shook the dry bones" of the "fashionable" young ladies. It began with a prayer group of twenty and spread to the town where people from all walks of life jammed the uncompleted new brick church. Prominent citizens and their servants "came forward as mourners."[59] Reverberations from the outpouring were felt as far away as Marengo County in Alabama and Ouachita Parish in Louisiana. At the end of the year the membership roll of the conference passed over the mark of ten thousand whites and three thousand blacks.[60]

Pittsburgh hosted the General Conference in 1828. The Mississippi delegates gleefully laid the fruits of their four years of labor upon the altar of Yankee statisticians. The grand total had now topped the twenty-thousand level. Knowing that the southern-minded Soule had largely inspired the primitive zeal of these backwoodsmen to perform evangelical miracles, the New England keepers of the altar brought heresy charges against the bishop for a tract he had published and distributed through the Methodist Book Concern. It was the Mississippians who led the fight to forestall a nasty ecclesiastical trial.[61]

After returning *via* steamboat to "Happy Valley," they launched the second phase of their campaign. During the summer and autumn, camp meetings were conducted in the woods near Washington, at Tapisaw on the Pearl, Adams Settlement, Bethel near Woodville, and in the Choctaw Nation. At the Bethel outing the Sunday congregation numbered from three to five thousand, scores of whom were openly converted. Some thirty new members were received into the church, most of whom were "very intelligent" young ladies who may have been chums of those converted during the recent revival at the Female Academy.[62]

Down in Mobile, Thomas Burpo's congregation was literally bursting the seams of the old "Hive" church. Several times the seating capacity was enlarged, and to provide "higher seats in the synagogue" for the blacks a gallery was added.[63] Over in New Orleans, the Methodists could at long last point with justifiable pride, especially to their Roman Catholic, Presbyterian, Baptist and Episcopalian friends,[64] to a fully organized, amply housed congregation of twenty or thirty whites and twice that number of blacks and "Cajuns." Two young converts, race unknown, were preparing to enter the traveling ministry by reading their assigned lessons prescribed by the Conference Course of Study.[65]

More than one hundred miles to the north, Alexander Talley and the elderly Isaac Smith, who never forsook their mission to the people of the forest, were immersed in a series of camp meetings. At one, fifty-two Indians, seven whites, and three blacks, possibly slaves of the LeFlores or David Folsom, were received into the church. Among the hundreds who "under great concern" were "overwhelmed, senseless, agonized," or who found "peace in believing," was a young Choctaw brave named William Winans Oakchiah. One year later the man who baptized him and for whom he was named recommended him for admission on trial in the traveling ministry—the first of his Nation to be ordained a Methodist elder.[66]

At the end of 1829 three thousand two hundred and forty-three Choctaw communicants shared the Lord's Supper with their white and black brothers and sisters.[67] Their feasting was destined soon to end in famine.

Early in 1830, Oakchiah's sponsor noted in a letter to a young physician named John Gibson that the "sapient" Mississippi Legislature had enacted a measure of profound Christian charity! She had granted to the Choctaw all citizenship rights save one: "the right of suffrage." Under the Constitution of 1817 this right was restricted to white male citizens of the state. The constitutionality of the act was unassailable; the motivation for it was unconscionable. Lawmakers had simply fashioned a statutable cudgel to drive the Choctaw from his lands in order for their white constituents to move in with their black work force and exploit that fruitful virgin soil in the name of King Cotton.[68]

Ten days later the same writer addressed William Lattimore, a prominent physician and politician, who maintained that the Indian bill carefully guaranteed the Choctaw his "Natural Rights."[69] The country preacher suggested that the doctor should stick to his last and refrain from dabbling in moral theology. Garbed in their finest biblical robes, legislators had simply failed to get a good Greek reading of the injunction in Titus 3:2. They had acted more like truant boys who suddenly realized that the "watermelons they were devouring were not their own."[70]

Next on the preacher's letter list was Edmund Smith, an Amite County legislator and neighbor. The two men often conversed at the post office in Centreville, and were usually in complete accord on matters political. But Smith had now lost his bearings and had endorsed a grievous crime against the red man—a crime which could ultimately result in the dissolution of "every political institution" of the Republic. These priceless republican institutions, founded on the doctrine of human rights, would, if violated, turn on the despoiler and sever the "moral ties which bind our society together." If in fact legislative halls in Jackson were not a den of thieves, they were indeed glutted with hypocrites who had stamped upon the political character of the commonwealth "a stigma which neither time nor future rectitude" could erase.[71]

The Mississippi Methodists were called upon to hit the campaign trail, defy the demagogue, demand a constitutional convention,[72] counter the "subtle and violent" mischief of speculators and lawyers, and arouse the electorate from their apathy. But public apathy was the politicians' happy hunting ground. They pitched their "refreshment tents" at camp meetings[73] to foster this apathy, persuade inept yeomen to cast their ballots for land-hungry democratizers, and defy visionary preachers who advocated racial amalgamation with the red man. It reminded the Wesleyan evangelist of entrepreneurs who had hawked doves in the Court of the Gentiles.[74]

By the time virgin forest trees began to display their golden glory, it was too late for tears. Protest meetings against the nefarious designs of demagogues in Jackson and Washington were strangely shunned by weak-kneed preachers and laymen. They reminded one champion of the Choctaw of those who shouted loudest against Demon Rum during camp meetings, but staggered to the polls to vote dry. Politicians, planters and preachers who could "invade wantonly the rights of a single savage man" would "sell the universe" for a few pieces of silver.[75]

Thomas Griffin[76] and others publicly protested legislative action "so *unworthy* of a *moral* people." Caroline Mathilda Thayer, headmistress of the Female Academy, called an emergency meeting of nabob matrons to draft a "Remonstrance" addressing the issue.[77] But by this time the Treaty of Dancing Rabbit Creek was being initialed,[78] and emigrations to Arkansas had begun.[79] By Thanksgiving Day the conference journal noted "quite a shadow over our prospects."[80] Withdrawing to the shadows of his forest domain, Oakchiah waited a year for his day to dawn.

Three: Defenders Against the Yankee Threat

What . . . can the Slave-holding States do? Let them make the best they can of their unfavorable circumstances. Let them cling to the Union and the Constitution.

William Winans

Six years before a band of gloomy preachers rode out from Tuscaloosa toward Choctaw villages soon to fade away forever, the great Chief Pushmataha had prophesied in the presence of the Marquis de Lafayette: "We shall soon be in the land of shadows."[1] Conscience-smitten and downcast for their failure to close ranks in defense of the red man's natural right to life, liberty, property and the pursuit of happiness under God, white men cut foresquare from Wesleyan moral cloth determined to dispel the lengthening shadows and restore the sun of hope in the hearts of a dispossessed people.[2]

One year later these men rode in to Woodville with pine tar on their boots to meet with their "Frontier Bishop," Robert R. Roberts. The shadows were gone, lost in the light of eyes fixed upon high resolve. Talley had returned to his people, and the stalwart John Cotton had joined him to do battle with the whiskey peddlers.[3] Moses Perry had married a devout Choctaw maiden and cast his lot with the Nation. William Winans Oakchiah had cast his lot with white brothers.

For ten long days—exceptionally long for frontier annual conferences—the exhausted bishop and his men hammered away at the mountainous tasks that would test the mettle of their future mission. As pragmatic learners from hard lessons, they profited immeasurably from their fractured response to the state's intimidation, deception and demoralization of the Choctaw.[4] For one thing, they had learned that disorganized moral forces courted disaster, and they resolved to tighten every bolt of their organizational structure. For another, they now fully realized the high importance of cultivating the public mind for a rational response to the merits of their cause. The result was a determination to initiate an educational venture intended to reach far beyond the scope of common schools and the confined campus of a college for young ladies.[5]

One highlight of the Woodville sessions was an announcement that the American Colonization Society had appropriated $2,400 for Talley's work in Arkansas.[6] Another high point was the decision, subject to confirmation by the General Conference of 1832, to provide the resources for the support of an autonomous annual conference in Alabama.[7] Mississippi was prepared to transfer thirty-eight of her eighty traveling preachers, 8,196 of her 14,576 white and 2,770 of her 5,415 black constituents to the care of the new jurisdiction. The seven hundred and one Indians were to remain with the mother conference. Similar plans were being formulated for a new conference designated Memphis astride the Mississippi-Tennessee line.[8]

If some practical jokester like "Tommy" Owens had posted a sign outside the conference room it might have read "Caution: Men at Work!"[9] But he would have been more of a prophet than a prankster. He and his colleagues were resolutely committed to this one thing: to expand Gibson's beachhead to new frontiers where white men and the black labor force were moving in to exploit the land. By the time the Chickasaw ceded his land to the state in the Treaty of Pontotoc on October 22, 1832, the shift of political and economic power from the old Natchez region to the piney woods had already begun.[10]

Caught up in the feverish ferment of Jacksonian Democracy, settlers in the new lands were not about to defer to the Natchez Junto, "the nearest thing to a political machine in the state."[11] If this meant that Methodist men were expected to play rough at the tough game of politics, they were ready and able to join the fray. Most of them were convinced that nothing in their religious creed justified their exclusion from either political activism or public office. Yet many of their constituents suspected "a religious establishment from seeing a clergyman elevated to the office of constable!" To this quip the preachers replied: An intelligent constable could better read the public mind than an ignorant governor![12]

They elected seven of their most intellectually inclined colleagues to represent them at Philadelphia in 1832. They were instructed to confer with Wilbur Fisk, a graduate of Brown and president of Wesleyan University in Middletown, Connecticut,[13] and commissioned to offer him a similar post in a liberal arts college for men in Mississippi, then in the planning stage. Although they anticipated little if any success in their offer, their higher purpose was to invade the exclusive territory of Yankee ivy-league schools and thus arrest the attention of intellectuals at Philadelphia. In this way they hoped to alter eastern images of "ignoramuses" preaching to slave-beating settlers in the piney woods.

This was the "new look" which Roberts discussed at length with his men at Woodville. In a much less sophistical move, he and his cabinet deliberately challenged a cherished educational institution of the Methodist itineracy: the Course of Study.[14] Previously limited to two years of biblical and ascetical studies with one examination at the end of the second year, the course of Mississippi was extended to four years with examinations annually. Yale and Andover divines were highly amused that country preachers could excite such a storm of controversy over their quest for "edication" that it would threaten their quest with schism during the ensuing decade.[15]

A young graduate of Washington College named John Emory was elected a bishop at Philadelphia.[16] Popular as the "Yankee Bishop" with strong southern feelings, he made his only visitation to Mississippi in 1833. He was among friends who supported his candidacy. He lauded their progressive action in extending and enhancing the Course of Study. He reminded his men that the rising generation of Mississippians, educated in institutions of higher learning at Oakland College in Lorman and Mississippi College in Clinton, would pay little heed to the preaching of Methodist "ignoramuses."[17]

During his stay in Natchez he encouraged preachers and leading laypersons to press on in their plans for "a male school of high grade" within the bounds of the conference, preferably located in the vicinity of the state capital. Members of the Natchez Junto were not, apparently, pleased by his suggestion. Nonetheless, although five years were to transpire before Centenary College was founded at Brandon Springs in Rankin County, the concept was not allowed to die, even in the dark days of the Panic of 1837.[18]

At the moment the more pressing matter concerned the need for a thorough overhauling of the conference structure. In many respects it had remained virtually unchanged for two decades. Radical demographic changes had occurred since the formation of the conference in 1813 and the Constitutional Convention four years afterward. The progressive bishop warned his men that the business of mission could no longer be conducted at "the same old stand." Adaptability had been a Wesleyan watchword since Oxford days. Consequently, he laid down new guidelines they were to implement before he returned for a strict accounting. New districts, circuits and missions were to be formed in Mississippi and Louisiana; older ones were to be named for towns and post offices rather than ridges and bayous and creeks. He projected the possibility that the population of the state would more than double during the decade—a prediction confirmed by the census of 1840.[19]

Bishop Emory caught the steamer at Natchez never to return. He was fatally injured in a buggy accident in 1835. By that time his Natchez friends had begun to feel the threat of another potential catastrophe to which he had alerted them during his sojourn among them: the abolitionist crusade.

While the Choctaw was being exiled to his American Babylon, Mississippians who read eastern papers were beginning to find William Lloyd Garrison's Boston *Liberator* in their mail boxes. Subscribers who had previously received copies of his bankrupt *Genius of Universal Emancipation* were initially amused by his zeal to beat a dead horse.[20] Older members of the defunct Franklin Debating and Library Society, which convened regularly at Jackson Academy in 1815, recalled that one of Garrison's predecessors named George Bourne had been unfrocked by the Virginia Presbytery for unkindly words about slaveholders.[21] Perhaps, they mused, the Great Yankee Liberator would fare no better.

The fiery Bostonian was loathe to do his homework. Had he bothered to investigate the facts he would have discovered that Mississippians in general and Methodists in particular had for decades held firm antislavery views. Five years before his birth in 1805 a pioneer scientist named Sir William Dunbar had declared that "Slavery could only be defended perhaps on the principle of expediency."[22] In 1818 the Supreme Court of Mississippi had pronounced a dictum worthy of his own editorial pen: "Slavery is condemned by reason and the laws of nature."[23] Ten years later Governor Gerald C. Brandon had enunciated the same antislavery principle in his public statement that "Slavery is an evil at best."[24]

In the light of his incredibility as an objective journalist, Garrison's crusade gathered little more than moss among Mississippi Methodists until Yankee preachers began to stir up "ill feeling and strife on the subject of negro slavery."[25] Tolerating the tirades of an "outsider" was one thing; indulging the moral diatribes of a Christian brother was quite another thing. The likelihood that a slaveholding preacher from Wilkinson County would ever join the Bostonian for a debate on the Commons was at best farfetched. The probability that he would presently be sitting across the aisle from an abolitionist disciple during the upcoming General Conference at Cincinnati in 1836 was a virtual certainty.[26]

If, as it seemed likely, the slaveholder and the abolitionist were to request recognition before the supreme council of the church to plead their antithetical causes, a cardinal tenet of Wesleyan doctrine would be subjected to the acid test: "If we are united, what can stand before us? If we divide, we shall destroy ourselves."[27]

In November prior to the Cincinnati conclave Bishop Soule arrived for conference with his men at Woodville. In his weathered valise he had packed a ponderous moral burden. He dispensed with routine matters of business posthaste, then sat down informally and dispassionately shared his weighty thoughts with them on the gravest threat confronting the church and the commonwealth: the institution of slavery.

He opened his informal dialogue with them in a tribute to one of their deceased moral giants, Alexander Talley, who had succumbed to cholera during the year. He then reminded them that the fruits of Talley's labors among the people of the forest had essentially been destroyed by the moral equivocation of white brethren who had failed to close ranks in defense of the red man's natural rights.[28]

Arrested by this disarming appeal to their consciences, they instinctively drew the moral parallel: if they were united in defense of the black man's destiny, what power on earth would be able to stand before them? Yet upon what moral principle must they take their united stand? Was it to be on the side of the land-hungry slaveholder who was prepared to retain his human chattels in perpetual chains, or was it to stand steadfastly with the abolitionist who cried out for immediate emancipation of slaves to live tenuous lives in the white community? Or was it possible to pursue a course of action morally superior in its consequences than either of these alternatives?

For several days the bishop and his men wrestled with their dilemma. Prior to adjournment a resolution was unanimously adopted which defined the position they were to assume for the next quarter of a century: to follow in the footsteps of Tobias Gibson, continue to preach the Gospel to master and slave alike, and cultivate the cultural climate for the eventual manumission of all blacks for colonization in their fatherland on the southern coast of Liberia. In the eyes of Yankee "intermeddlers" this may have been a "sinful" course to pursue, but none could deny that it was "practical," or "Methodistical."[29]

This document was immediately printed as a broadside and widely distributed across the river counties. Within a brief span previous shades of suspicion that the preachers were in collusion with their abolitionist brethren began to dissipate. Access to slave families for purposes of pastoral care was made easier, plantation gates once locked against the missionaries were flung open, and planters began to pay rather handsome stipends to the preachers for their ministrations. Whether or not this was open-faced paternalism or laudable evangelism was a determination which moral theologians and cultural historians continue to debate in vain.[30]

Three of the bishop's confidants were elected to

represent the conference at the Cincinnati conclave in April 1836: Benjamin Michael Drake, John Lane, and William Winans. Drake was a "great friend of education," Lane was a "gentleman" planter-preacher of moderate antislavery convictions, and Winans was a presiding elder of exceptional organizational and oratorical ability who considered slavery an insufferable blight on mankind. During the leisurely cruise to the Ohio metropolis they discussed the frightful possibility that the nation might soon become "a divided people, exposed to all the horrors of neighbor-warfare" made all the more horrible by "the feeling of fraternal hatred" among Methodists over the burning issue of slavery.[31]

For the moment, they concluded, the singular hope for the preservation of the Union, the unity of Methodism, and the ultimate liberation of the black man was through the work of the American Colonization Society. Although the nationwide interfaith movement was officially endorsed by the Methodist Church, its principles and procedures were anathematized by Yankee abolitionist preachers and southern slaveholders alike. Its work would have cut the heart out of the abolition crusade for immediate emancipation; it threatened planters as a possible actuator of slave insurrections.[32] The men from Mississippi feared that at Cincinnati the warring partisans might crush the hopes of the movement in the pincers of a violent public polemic.

Much to their relief, this distressing possibility was fortunately avoided. According to local press reports it was Mississippi men who stood tallest during the floor debate, probably forestalling a disaster. After the position paper drafted at Woodville had been read and explained by Drake, the principle it espoused was adopted by a vote of nine to one.[33] When Orange Scott, the leading abolitionist in the New England Conference, challenged the moral integrity of the Mississippi position, reporters commented that he had been subjected to a flurry of "flagellations" by the slaveholding Winans.[34] When the time arrived for the election of bishops, the Mississippi delegation threw its full weight behind Wilbur Fisk, a native Vermonter, and Thomas A. Morris, a Westerner.[35]

Totally committed to the cause of higher education, Fisk civilly declined his election to the high office. His southern supporters were deeply disappointed, for his moderate views on slavery were widely known across their land. His influence would have gone "far towards quieting the dissatisfaction" of concerned planters with the announced aims of the Colonization Society. They feared that its reputed collusion with abolitionists would ultimately result in a concerted assault upon their plantation enclaves.[36]

By the time Bishop Morris came to Vicksburg for conference in December 1836, anti-abolition emotion had reached a feverish level across the state.[37] "Outsiders" were becoming suspect, but the new bishop was not shunned. As a former editor of the *Western Christian Advocate,* a seasoned itinerant who demonstrated "superiority of judgment," and a man whose "educational and religious qualifications" were "without fault," he had become "a great favorite" with Mississippi laymen and preachers. High on his agenda of business was the pressing problem of manpower, without which the most ambitious plans for missionary outreach would have been impossible to accomplish.

The bishop's anxiety was dispelled by the goodly number of men at Vicksburg available for work. Eleven were admitted on trial, four were ordained deacons and four had graduated to elder's orders. Sixteen local preachers were ordained deacon and elder to replace the departed Randall Gibson and other "oldtimers." Augmenting the corps were two Indians, Oakchiah and Toblychubby, and several blacks including Gloster (Gloucester) Simpson and Pompey. Simpson had recently visited the colony in

Liberia, and Pompey was left free to continue preaching to his own people and whites, by whom he was "highly respected and popular," often being "invited into their homes" to break bread with them.[38]

Two years later Morris returned for conference at Grenada, where only recently red men had pitched their wigwams. A new map of the conference boundaries, drawn following the Battle of San Jacinto in the previous April, had been temporarily tacked on the log wall for his perusal. In land mass, Texas dominated the amateur cartographer's handiwork. Prompted by this graphic exposé of a vast virgin domain ripe for the Gospel, the bishop selected his timely Sunday sermon text from Daniel 12:4. As they listened to his stirring missionary words, the preachers envisioned the day when "pure Arminianism" would spread across this land of promise. Planters present for the ordination rites dreamed of the day when they would move in with their slaves to exploit its boundless blessings.[39]

Slaveholding preachers in the audience were unable to avoid the anguish of their moral dilemma. It was destined to deepen painfully during the ensuing decade.

Whether justified or not, Mississippi Methodists devoted that tenuous interim to tasks that belied their moral stature. They reenforced their modest forces for the lamentable day when they would part ways with their northern brethren. Like Daniel of old, they were resolved "at that time" to "be delivered" from the Yankee threat to their moral integrity as Christian brothers. Reluctantly, but resolutely, the Mississippi delegates arrived at Baltimore for the General Conference of 1840 with a portfolio of facts and figures to support their position.[40]

During the quadrennium the Mississippi Conference had extended her moral influence over western Alabama, set the Memphis Conference upon her independent course, pressed deeper into Louisiana and provided itinerants for the new Texas mission. Missionary work on the plantations and in the Chickasaw Purchase was rapidly expanding, new churches were being built in town and country, and Centenary College had been founded at Brandon Springs and was in full operation.[41] Poydras Street Church in New Orleans had been dedicated, and a mission had finally been organized in Jackson, Mississippi, near the Old Capitol. Conference membership had more than kept pace with the population explosion, and the Panic of 1837 had been weathered with aplomb.[42]

Abolitionists were not impressed with their story. Methodist leaders of the movement in New England—Orange Scott, Gerrit Smith, LaRoy Sunderland[43]—accused their Mississippi peers of gobbling up territories and imposing their will on the inhabitants for one purpose alone: to defend against outside forces bent on liberating the slave.

The Scott clique suspected that "The Mississippi Story" of evangelical expansionism was a public relations screen thrown up to protect a slaveholding enclave determined to establish an autonomous southern *ecclesia*. Smith lambasted efforts to build a "heathen" church in New Orleans.[44] When news reached Baltimore that on May 7 the church in Natchez had been extensively damaged by a killer tornado, he apparently refused to contribute to its rebuilding.[45] Scott excoriated Mississippi preachers for alleged complicity with judges in the enforcement of state statutes limiting the testimony of blacks in civil cases against white defendants.[46]

At times the floor debates became inflammatory. But in the end the efforts of abolitionists to condemn Mississippians for connivance with vested slaveholding interests were soundly defeated. At the same time their Yankee friends refused to consider any Southerner for election as bishop. Undeterred by this open denial of their constitutional rights, they resolved that nothing would inhibit their preaching of the Gospel to master and slave alike.[47]

It was an open secret that Scott and his partisans had singled out James Osgood Andrew,[48] the only southern-born bishop, as their prime target for an assault on Methodist slaveholders generally. To discredit and depose him would have been an abolitionist *coup* indeed. But their charges against him were suspect, so that little more than exchanges of empty rhetoric resulted from the Baltimore sessions.

Six months later Andrew arrived at Vicksburg for annual conference. Praised as "one of us . . . identified with all Southern interests, and acquainted with all our Southern institutions,"[49] he was heartened in his resolve to turn the tables on his Yankee adversaries and their grandiloquent words of concern for the dispossessed. His first act was to admit James Naconchia, a full-blooded Choctaw, into the itinerant ministry.[50] He then turned the full focus of the conference on the needs of the black people. He instructed a committee to prepare a catechism for the religious instruction of children irrespective of race. He licensed several black men to preach, and gave free rein to Thomas Clinton to cover Wilkinson County as plantation evangelist. Notwithstanding a state statute forbidding missionaries to teach young blacks to read and write, the bishop insisted that Clinton and others save minds as well as souls.[51]

With this cardinal Wesleyan principle Scott could find no fault. Then the bishop committed an unforgivable sin: he married a slaveholding spouse from Georgia. Now the abolitionists had a legitimate case against their defiant brother, and they made capital of it during the General Conference at Greene Street Church in New York City in 1844. By that time their case against him had snowballed into a nationwide *cause célèbre.*[52]

Mississippi men mustered their moral and material forces in preparation for the mountain that threatened to fall upon them. Had they been men of lesser stature they would have given in to defeat. They might have abandoned the Texas mission, aborted the opening of Centenary College,[53] and consigned New Orleans to the Devil following the death of Elijah Steele, who had stuck to his post during the ravaging epidemic of yellow fever in 1841.[54] They might even have rawhided their defenseless blacks into abject submission, or, like the red man, exiled them to the wastelands of a distant West to rid themselves of the cause of their miserable dilemma.

With no such thoughts on their minds, the preachers rode in to Woodville for conference on a freezing November day of 1843. They refused to take "refuge in a dream world" like many of their people and clerical peers in other communions.[55] When Daniel DeVinne informed them from New York that "all of the concessions have been made to the South which will ever be made,"[56] their unexpected response was moderate and conciliatory. They called for an extraordinary churchwide conference of knowledgeable leaders to discuss their common concerns and dispel their grievances; to seek peace and unity, not war and dissolution. To this call, both Soule and Andrew affixed their blessing.[57]

Moreover, the two bishops had arranged for New York's Edmund Storer Janes to address the Woodville gathering.[58] He lauded the nobility of Mississippi's call for an *ad hoc* conference of conciliation, and before departing he met privately with Edward McGehee and other laypersons, as well as delegates to the upcoming General Conference, to discuss strategy. The substance of their talks was deliberately destroyed by the secretary, Samuel W. Speer, as history's secret. But it is no secret that Benjamin M. Drake nominated Janes for bishop during the General Conference. Abolitionists would probably have anathematized one of their own persuasion for nominating a Mississippi slaveholding

53

preacher for election to the College of Bishops. In his nominating speech Drake apparently implied as much.[59]

For sixteen days and nights in May of 1844 one hundred and eighty delegates sat in Greene Street Church awaiting the dreaded moment of truth. From the seventeenth to June eighth the unrelenting gears of dissolution ground to an horrendous halt. By a vote of one hundred and thirty-six to fifteen, division was declared a *fait accompli*.[60] Precisely why American Methodism was torn asunder is a question which historians continue to probe with little hope of success. Whether or not the breach was caused by slavery, or sectionalism, or old-fashioned sin, or a combination of all, remains a moot question. But for Mississippians the consequences remain to this day.

Their delegates to New York claimed to have "shrunk, with horror, from the idea of *Separation*" until the final moment of the "fatal collision." Before taking leave of the city they led in the formation of a southern task force whose purpose was to explain to their constituents precisely what had happened in the anterooms of the tormented conference. Their mission was to prove as distasteful as it was hopeless.[61]

Garbled reports had reached Mississippi and Louisiana suggesting that Drake, Lane and Winans had meekly bowed to the dictates of the Yankees. Moreover, it was rumored that war was imminent, and that a slave insurrection was being organized by the abolitionists in concert with the Colonization Society. Fearing that he was a party to the conspiracy, police in New Orleans arrested William H. Watkins for preaching to the blacks in Moreau Street Church. So aroused were the people of Needham B. Raiford's China Grove congregation that they called a mass meeting to boycott any preacher appointed by "a bishop not in sympathy with Bishop Andrew." Similar protest meetings were conducted in Natchez, Vicksburg and Houma.[62]

On arriving home, Mississippi's task force promptly tackled its assignment. Covering every possible trouble spot, the members explained how in their efforts to forestall the disaster they had borne the "outrages" of Yankee "Jesuitism" with Christian grace. Janes and others commended them for behavior becoming a true Wesleyan. From other northern brethren came words of "respect and sympathy." Raiford and his flock should take this example to heart; recrimination, vituperation and inflammatory language only lowered them to the level of abolitionists.[63]

Serious questions arose as to whether or not Bishop Janes should come for conference at Port Gibson in December following the New York conclave. But he never hesitated. He found a weary and harassed corps of clergy—weary after a devastating flood and a violent outbreak of yellow fever; harassed by rebellious congregations. Their conference hosts, the Presbyterians, were dismayed by their "captious" behavior. Yet when a unanimous vote favoring the Plan of Separation was announced, no rebel yells disturbed the quiet of the sanctuary. With the calm characteristic of his breed, the bishop shared their sorrow for those lost in the epidemic. He absolved them of any dereliction of duty. He assured them that if he chose not to go with the South, it would be solely for the purpose of influencing a "favorable intercourse" between separated brethren.[64]

Strictly adhering to the rules laid down in the plan, delegates from the southern conferences convened at Louisville, Kentucky, in May 1845 to organize a new ecclesiastical jurisdiction. Winans, and perhaps others, went reluctantly, fearing scenes "even more trying than that at New York."[65] Convention proceedings confirmed the reasons for their anxiety. A power struggle for control of the episcopacy had developed between the Seaboard and southwestern conferences. Sharp divisions over strategy in the defense of slavery had surfaced. No consensus on any vital issue of ecclesiastical or ideological nature was reached during the convention sessions. Any image of a "solid" Southern Methodism was grossly distorted.[66]

One year later the first General Conference of the Methodist Episcopal Church, South, convened in a predominantly black church in Petersburg, Virginia.[67] Unabashed politicking was rampant. Limpid efforts at dispassionate deliberation were further frustrated by bizarre abuse from the northern secular and religious press. Thomas E. Bond's New York *Christian Advocate and Journal* accused Winans of high crimes and misdemeanors ranging from perjury to treason for his role in the debates of 1844.[68] Even Henry Clay, a Whig casualty of the sectional wars, suspected that separation had set the pattern for the future dissolution of the Union of States.[69]

In an artless move to stymie the election of Winans to the episcopacy, Seaboard delegates nominated his protégé, Drake, to siphon off his support. They then turned and elected William Capers of South Carolina and Robert Paine of Tennessee, by-passing Mississippians altogether,[70] although Paine was born and raised in Aberdeen, Mississippi.[71] Equally ironical to Winans was the fact that he was hastily called from the sessions to address a mass meeting of the New York Colonization Society in New York City.[72]

After creating an annual conference in Louisiana[73]—possibly engineered to dilute Mississippi's power base in the lower South—the maiden conference adjourned. Mississippians happily returned to their mission at home where defenses against Yankee meddling and Seaboard politicking were more securely implanted. Now, so they thought, they would be free from polemics in high places. Summer and autumn were "unusually healthy," but the cotton crop was short. The first class of five graduated from Centenary, but the Female Academy was on the verge of closing her doors forever. Two preachers defected to the North, but six others deserted their posts because "the people would not support them." The only good report was "the work with colored people."[74]

Their white flocks seemed more concerned with the outcome of the Wilmot Proviso and Henry Clay's defeat than in winning souls to Christ.[75] Hypocritical congregations refused to provide their preachers with parsonages, but subjected their wives to vicious gossip. Yet had traveling preachers been deterred from their mission by political strife and sewing-circle hearsay, they would not willingly have given over eight thousand of their white and more than thirty-three hundred of their black members to the care of the new Louisiana Conference.[76] They would probably have left Centenary to gather chaff in Rankin County rather than relocating her on the campus of vacated Louisiana College at Jackson, and never called Augustus Baldwin Longstreet to her presidency. His son-in-law, Lucius Quintus Cincinnatus Lamar, may never have been accorded an honored place among Mississippi's "Heroes."[77]

Had an obscure teacher named John Spencer been cut from less durable moral cloth, he may not have converted his old field school into a training cadre for leaders in church and state during the years of war and Reconstruction. Reuben Webster Millsaps, who later graduated from DePauw University in Indiana, may never have laid the foundation for Millsaps College forty years afterward.[78] John J. Wheat, who became a Methodist preacher and studied theology at Princeton, may never have taught Greek at the University of Mississippi.[79]

While Spencer was busy nurturing a new generation to walk tall into an uncertain future, Methodists along the Ohio were engaged in ecclesiastical strife that somehow presaged a more deadly one to come.[80] Along the banks of the beautiful river entire communities were torn apart over matters of property "till charity wept."[81] Reconciliation between separated brethren virtually dissipated as a hope when a stalwart preacher from the red hills of Georgia named Lovick Pierce dispatched an official letter of "Christian regards and fraternal salutations" to the General Conference of the Northern Church at Pittsburgh in 1848.[82]

Five days after his credentials as "Fraternal Delegate" were presented, the conference resolved that it was not "proper, at present, to enter into fraternal relations with the Methodist E. Church, South."[83] Boston's *Zion's Herald* promptly added: "Let it go forth that the Methodist Episcopal Church rejects all alliances with pro-slavery ecclesiastical bodies."[84] One month later a Mississippi preacher wrote to an Illinois physician: "I feel that their course is disgraceful to Methodism—not so much an injury to the South, as an ineffaceable stigma on the character of Northern Methodists. Thank God, my connection, with men who could act thus, had ceased ere the acts had been perpetrated."[85]

One historian rather convincingly suggests that Pierce's letter was designed as a provocation.[86] Others disagree.[87] At the moment Mississippi preachers and laity considered its rejection an unpardonable if not final disposition of any hope that The People Called Methodists would again be one. From that moment they were faced with no alternative but to prepare their moral forces to resist further assaults upon their enclave, draw in the flanks of their front-line troops and walk tall toward the trenches.

In their patience they "contained their soul" and went about their mission with relative calm. Evidence of fire-eating activism among them is scant. While many of their Protestant peers clamored for Secession, they cried for more laborers, "especially in Missions to people of Colour." As veterans of frontier battles with Satan, they went "without hesitation to their tasks." With no permanent place to call home, their wives were caught up in an endless round of packing and moving on, following the old custom of visiting with their husbands around the circuits.[88]

Unnamed and unsung local preachers moved from plantation to plantation, preaching to slaves and masters and teaching their children to read and write. Sunday schools proliferated at the grass roots. Classes at Pine Ridge were limited to six students each, and they were required "to walk orderly" and not leave their benches without teacher's permission. Discipline was the watchword for the rising generation which would inevitably be confronted with agonizing moral choices during the fateful fifties and sixties.[89]

New schools for their Christian nurture were being founded or planned by John Harvie at Port Gibson, by Pleasant J. Eckles at Sharon and Benjamin Holt in Carroll County.[90] And at Pleasant Valley a memorable revival "rolled over the field" like a "tidal wave" for a month.[91] During the storm to come, Yankees would have difficulty drowning out shouts of glory.

Four: Survivors of the Eye of the Storm

If the Lord of hosts had not left us a few survivors, we should have been like Sodom, and become like Gomorrah.

Isaiah 1:9

On December 5, 1849, Bishop William Capers called the Mississippi Conference to order in the town of Natchez.[1] Forty-eight hours earlier the first session of the Thirty-first Congress had convened on Capitol Hill. Separated as they were by a thousand miles, the two bodies of men were confronted by a common, ominous threat: "a dark augury of the storms to come."[2] Politicians and preachers shared one distressing thought: that the extension of slavery to new territories might expose church and state to the desolating force of a killer tornado lurking on the national horizon.

The circuit riders had survived violent storms in the past. Once again they were mustering their forces to withstand "The Impending Crisis,"[3] but the warning trumpets were giving out "an uncertain sound." In previous crises they had usually stood shoulder-to-shoulder. But since separation from Mother Church and the creation of their own southern communion, internecine conflicts had gravely exposed their fractured flanks to the mercies of any storm which might beat against their house.

Recent political events had further polarized the members of their household. To the delight of the Whigs among them, William Winans had recently challenged the Democratic incumbent from the Fourth Mississippi Congressional District, Albert Gallatin Brown, for his seat. Brown's Methodist partisans scorned their brother for exposing the chinks in the popular congressman's radical proslavery shield. During the autumn campaign of 1849 Woodville Democrats boycotted religious services conducted by the Whig candidate. On hearing of this affront to a brother, Augustus B. Longstreet, a dyed-in-the-wool Democrat, casually offered his condolences to the country preacher from "Elysian Fields."[4]

In a less jocular dialogue the two seasoned veterans of the ecclesiastical wars were in complete agreement on one point: Mississippi preachers had permitted their abolitionist brethren to define the cardinal issue of the time: slavery. They had simply stranded themselves in a moral and tactical *cul-de-sac*. They had committed the sin of political sins. They had created, albeit inadvertently, the climate for schism in the church. They were now unwilling participants in the pending crucifixion of the Union of the States.[5]

Beyond this consensus the two preachers agreed to disagree. Longstreet contended that the only possible course of escape from the eye of the storm was for the South to secede from the Union, cultivate a cosmetic black sub-culture on the plantations, and secure southern institutions against the voices of dissent within and without.[6] Winans insisted that the South should "cling to the Union and the Constitution," gradually prepare the slave for emancipation, and extend slavery to the new territories only if and when their citizens, on attaining statehood, should concur.[7] In the end both courses of escape were barricaded by the bodies of boys from the wheat fields of the Great Plains and the cotton fields of Dixie.

Neither statesmen nor churchmen succeeded in holding back the storm. On May 8, 1850, the Congress began debating the "Omnibus Bill," one of five composing the Compromise proposed by Henry Clay addressing the issue of slavery in the territories.[8] On that same day the General Conference of the Southern Methodist Church was in session at Saint Louis during an epidemic of cholera. Problems and potentials for mission in the new lands directly affected by the Clay Resolutions were necessarily discussed in great haste if not in an atmosphere of near-panic.[9]

The five Mississippi delegates had once again, as at Louisville, come reluctantly. As expected, they were presently stunned by the inflammatory rhetoric of the Episcopal Address apparently masterminded by Capers. It was saturated with anti-northern and proslavery allusions "hardly designed to encourage peace and understanding." It drove a deeper wedge between separated brethren currently engaged in a violent border property paper war. It further alienated the Seaboard partisans of Capers and Randolph-Macon's William A. Smith from Mississippi moderates committed to the maintenance of "peace and harmony."[10]

The image of Mississippi Fire-Eaters in parson's attire should have been at least partially corrected by Winans' carefully worded conciliatory address rebutting the "radical" posture of the Virginians and Carolinians. Although Mississippians esteemed Henry Bidleman Bascom for his untiring labors on behalf of African Colonization, they considered his election as bishop nothing short of tragic.[11] He was pathologically anti-northern. Drake would have been the better choice, but then he had no propaganda voice like the *Richmond Christian Advocate* and the *Southern Christian Advocate* of Charleston to advance his candidacy.

Except for the brief appearance of John N. Maffitt's *Mississippi Christian Herald* during 1835, the Mississippi Conference had lacked a circulating house organ.[12] Convinced by events at Saint Louis that the time was ripe for a paper of their own, delegates boarded the *James Hewitt*. En route home they launched the *New Orleans Christian Advocate* upon its way, with Drake acting as interim editor. On July

10, 1850, a "prospectus" came off the press, challenging Seaboard papers and the northern media to "sympathize with our views, understand our interests," or change to "meet our wants." The first regular edition, under the editorship of Holland N. McTyeire, pastor of New Orleans' Felicity Street Church, appeared on February 8, 1851.[13]

By that time the Mississippi preachers had resolved to withhold their support for the venture as a protest against McTyeire's "ultraism." Whigs among them feared that he might convert the paper into a partisan organ aimed at diluting the political influence of moderates such as Henry Clay and Henry Stuart Foote, Mississippi's last Whig governor and a fellow-Methodist.[14] In fact, when the governor was invited to address a Sunday night congregation in the Methodist Church of the capital city in January 1851,[15] Loco Foco papers and Democratic preachers protested that he was "out of place in the pulpit," and the pastor of the host church was roundly censured for having extended the invitation.[16]

In December following this donnybrook the Mississippi Conference convened in the capital city during the rebuilding of the local church. Although other denominations offered their facilities for the annual meeting, the Whig-controlled committee on arrangements was unable to resist the governor's offer of the Capitol for the sessions. But no Democratic voices were now heard to protest. None was raised when Drake, the soft-spoken Whig, presided at the speaker's podium in the House Chamber. Loco Focos were told that their martyred hero, Bishop Andrew, might be expected to appear at any moment to assume the gavel![17]

"Old Bullet" Longstreet quipped that only an imbecilic office seeker would continue to challenge the inherent influence of a hierarchy uniquely fashioned for political purposes. Circuit riders, presiding elders, bishops and local preachers serving grass-roots congregations were in constant contact with an electorate inclined to take political sermonizing seriously.[18] Shoutin' Methodists were a fact of political life.

During the sessions in chambers where legislators ordinarily sat and spat tobacco "chaws" into brass spittoons, Democrats, Whigs and Know-Nothings were exposed to a clinic in the techniques of swaying the masses. Whether planned with Foote's blessing or not, William H. Watkins stirred up an oldtime revival with dominant missionary overtones. Some eight souls were converted outright, the podium became the mourner's bench, and before the "awakening" had run its course seventy more souls "found peace in believing." Rival politicians on the stump knelt together and arose to open their pouches for an offering to mission to blacks, to red men they had exiled, to new settlers in California, and to the perishing multitudes of China across the sea.[19]

Then, on the eve of adjournment, Charles K. Marshall and Henry T. Lewis led a caravan of preachers and women into the rotunda to wage a holy war on Demon Rum. Lobbyists buttonholed legislators, demanding a law against "the two great potentates of the Western World: Whiskey and Brandy," the "ruin of all that is excellent in morals and government." After Foote had run at loggerheads with his legislature over its excessive secessionist posture, resigned his office and headed for California, his successor, John Jones McRae, signed a local option bill into law.[20]

Milling with the crowd during this Wesleyan Jubilee was a young graduate student of the University of Mississippi named James William Lambuth.[21] One year later, while continuing his studies in law and medicine, he began to sense that strange stirring of soul which his mentors, Longstreet, Lamar, and possibly John N. Waddell and Frederick A. P. Barnard, may have mentioned to him.[22] Aware of the lad's struggle with himself, Longstreet brought him along to conference at Canton in November 1853, during which Benjamin Jenkins spoke glowingly of his experiences as a missionary to China for five years.[23]

William and his Yankee bride of a month, Mary Isabella McClellan of New York, were captivated by Jenkins' appeal for helpers. Then and there they offered themselves for service in the Orient. Strong men knelt when he was admitted on trial, and their spouses wept when Mary placed an offering in the alms basin with a note reading: "I give five dollars and myself."[24] Two months after their arrival at Shanghai in 1854, Walter Russell was born to their union.[25]

Delegates to the General Conference at Columbus, Georgia, were apparently unmoved by the dramatic story Longstreet told. They were too immersed in contentious strife over the black man to heed the Macedonian cry of the yellow man. Proslavery zealots, confident that southern opinion had sufficiently crystallized since the appearance of Harriet Beecher Stowe's *Uncle Tom's Cabin* in 1851 to warrant a change in the *Discipline,* called for a positive statement: "Slavery was *not* an evil." Mississippi men refused to concur, and moderation prevailed. But, with the exception of an "oldtimer" from Virginia, John Early, they lost to two "city preachers" in the episcopal election: George Foster Pierce of Georgia, and Hubbard H. Kavanaugh of Kentucky.[26]

Moderation, however, was not the hallmark of mission in Mississippi during the ensuing quadrennium. Her schools were becoming burgeoning recruiting grounds for young men and women workers. Centenary's enrollment reach the 220 mark. Madison College, a non-sectarian school headed by Thomas C. Thornton, who had resigned his teaching post at Centenary, opened her doors to students in 1854. Whitworth College for young ladies was expected to receive her first class within four years.[27]

The campus was emerging as the choice site of revivals once thought to be the province of campgrounds.

When the elderly Early came for conference on Centenary's campus in November 1854 he quickly dispatched with business. He then plunged into a "protracted meeting," during which an outpouring of Pentecostal power shattered barriers separating Whigs and Democrats, Baptists and Presbyterians, blacks and whites. A sermon by Charles Taylor, missionary to China, so inspired the congregation that an offering of fifteen hundred dollars was received for young Lambuth and his wife. Months afterward, the revival was "still going on" across Feliciana Parish, and reaching up into the river counties of Mississippi.[28]

Planters praised the results of the awakening. Their slaves were not only being converted, but many of the plantation missions outdid the town congregations in contributions to the missionary cause in "heathen lands." Predominantly black congregations in the Fayette District contributed $1,205.40 of the $3,413.75 toward the support of Lambuth's mission. The offerings of non-Methodist planters, who welcomed the circuit riders and local preachers to their plantations, swelled the coffers of the conference. Mrs. Stowe would have had difficulty drowning out "the loud hozannas of these sable sons and daughters of Africa."[29]

Northern critics flailed Mississippi Methodists for segregating their black communicants in "reserved galleries." But only rarely, such as the dedication of the Kingston Church in 1857, were these "sable sons and daughters" summarily excluded from religious services. Indeed, in that year "free" sanctuaries were being constructed at Brunswick Landing, Magnolia, Port Gibson, Hazlehurst, Union and Hebron.[30] Moreover, not until Reconstruction were blacks provided separate physical facilities for worship.

For fourteen years the Southern Church had retained the original disciplinary rule forbidding "the buying and selling of men, women, and children, with the intention to enslave them." Then, during the General Conference at Nashville, Tennessee, in 1858, the controversial issue exploded with a passion. When the votes were counted, the rule was expunged. Seven months later the Mississippi Conference unanimously confirmed the action.[31] Winans and Lane, who had resisted the "radical" change, were dead; Drake was tottering toward his grave. Charles Kimball Marshall, an astute politician, had emerged as the conference leader.

The Vicksburg planter-preacher's influence on this abrupt turnabout cannot be discounted. It was a stroke of political genius. It left the Southern Church with no disciplinary rule on slavery to be debated. It caught Northern Methodists flatfooted. At least six of their annual conferences included substantial slaveholding constituencies who would have been read out of their church if their rule were strictly enforced. If their rule were relaxed or expunged, abolitionists waited in the wings to desolate their divided house.[32]

Suspended on the horns of this dilemma, they convened in Buffalo on May 16, 1860. While they were locked in debate over the disposition of their rule, news of Abraham Lincoln's nomination by the Chicago Convention arrived.[33] The answer to their quandary, they believed, lay in that terse news flash. An immediate vote was taken. The tellers announced that a majority had supported a revision of the rule to read: Slavery was a gross violation of "the laws of God and nature." Mississippians could now announce to the world that their northern brethren were members of "an 'anti-slavery' slaveholding Church"![34]

In November following Lincoln's nomination the Mississippi Conference convened in Natchez. During the sessions Governor John Jones Pettus called for a state convention to meet in January to decide the question of Secession. Marshall opened the convention with prayer, invoking heavenly powers against "mighty agencies" determined to deprive Mississippi of her "just rights, and destroying in our midst" the institution of slavery which "Providence has solemnly bound us to uphold, defend, and protect."[35]

"The die is cast—the Rubicon is crossed"! exclaimed James Lusk Alcorn.[36] Two days later the Act of Secession was announced "amid a silence so intense as to be oppressive," sighed the melancholy Lamar. Then, in a moment of defiant exultation men sprang to their feet and "saluted the first flag of the young republic" while ceremonial cannon belched balls of fire across the placid waters of the unpredictable Pearl.[37]

On April 12 unceremonious cannon flung balls of iron across the restless waters of Charleston Harbor. The "Splendid Pyrotechnic Exhibition" by dawn's early light drew droves of spectators who filled "every available space" along the breakwater.[38] In Macon, Mississippi, a rally around the courthouse square opened with prayer by a Baptist preacher who importuned The Almighty to bless the Confederacy, Jefferson Davis and the Noxubee Cavalry Squadron.[39] Down in Natchez old "Saratoga" probably blasted away across the Mighty Mississippi as she had done during the glorious days of "Tippecanoe" when Whig caperers danced in the streets.[40] But unlike his Baptist brother, the Wesleyan stalwart, John G. Jones, was never able "to pray in faith for the success of the Confederacy."[41]

Yet when Yankee raiders assaulted the barrier islands off Biloxi and their comrades in arms marched into Shiloh, Iuka, Oxford, Water Valley, Corinth and Holly Springs,[42] Jones was compelled to pray with members of his flock who marched off to war, and for his fellow itinerants who filled their quota of chaplains. The pacifism which swept their ranks eighty years later was virtually unknown among circuit riders in 1860.[43]

Wartime conferences in Mississippi bore no resemblance to Whig capers during the 1840s. Casualty lists turned the usual deliberations into lamentations. In 1861 John Jackson Millsaps, chaplain of John B. Floyd's brigade, died in Virginia following "an arduous campaign." John P. Richardson, chaplain of the 4th Mississippi, died a prisoner of war at Camp Chase on March 4, 1862. James Young Griffing, a preacher who volunteered as a private, was "loading and firing with marked precision" during the Battle of Antietam when he was felled by a bullet in the forehead.[44] David M. Wiggins, fifty-year-old presiding elder, resigned his post and was commissioned chaplain in the 30th Infantry. Returning exhausted to Sharon, he expired "quietly, without a groan or struggle."[45]

Only at the outset, 1861, did the conference endorse the war effort. Nothing—Lincoln's limited Proclamation of September 1862, or Grant's campaign against Vicksburg in November—compelled her to repeat the martial refrain. Preaching to the blacks became precarious, but missionaries remained undaunted in their efforts. Although churches were gutted by fire, schools were looted, and only three students remained in Centenary's collegiate department, the preachers stuck to their last. Even when the parsonage at Washington was converted into a hostel for Union officers, the conference refused to subscribe her good name for a second time to the Confederate Cause.[46]

If Secretary of War Edwin M. Stanton meant to bring Mississippi Methodists to their knees, nothing should have been more effective than his mandate placing their churches under the care of "loyal Clergy" appointed by "a loyal Bishop."[47] John P. Newman was placed in charge of "Ames Church" in New Orleans, renamed for Yankee Bishop Edward R. Ames.[48] After William H. Watkins had preached to a congregation in his Natchez Church, composed mainly of Union officers, he was threatened with removal and placed under house arrest for praying that God would "bless our enemies," but "give them the spirit of justice, humanity, and the fear of God!"[49]

Northern editors decried this "besotted, barbarous, brutalizing, bastard corruption and perversion of our holy religion."[50] But not a word in rebuttal appeared in the *New Orleans Christian Advocate.* Perhaps the reason for the paper's usual flight of editorial oratory being summarily silenced was simply the shortage of newsprint. Benjamin F. Butler's occupation of the port city following the bombardment by David G. Farragut's squadron virtually isolated it from the normal flow of supplies. Not only was freedom of the press thus effectively enforced, but the right of assembly was violated. Indeed, the General Conference scheduled to convene in the city during May 1862 was necessarily cancelled.[51]

This conclave was to have marked the golden jubilee of the founding of the Mississippi Conference. It was to have been a brief holiday for country preachers who had never gazed upon the wonders along Bourbon Street. It was to have celebrated a feast in memory of Elijah Steele who had snatched lost souls from the bars and brothels of the *Vieux Carré.* It was to have been a Day of Thanksgiving for God's gift of more than one hundred apostles of grace and more than twenty-seven thousand faithful souls now secure in His "everlasting arms" after fifty years of labor to send sons and daughters into Alabama, Louisiana, western Tennessee and Texas.[52] It was now an evangelical success story drowned out by martial drums "beating funeral marches to the grave."

For fragile spirits it was a sad consummation of fifty years of labor in vain. For persevering spirits it was a celebration of renewed resolve. Never before had they stood taller than in this hour, undismayed by the storms of war and devastation and deprivation. No cannon's "dread rattling thunder" could close their ears to the pleas of red men and black men and yellow men perishing in "outer darkness."[53]

William and Mary Lambuth personified this spirit of high resolve. In 1861 they came home on furlough, but the outbreak of hostilities cancelled their plans for an early return to the Orient. Yet after burying little Nellie, who died of scarlet fever, they felt compelled to venture as far as possible toward Mary's New York home and await overseas passage. Setting out from Madison County in a buggy and oxcart loaded with baggage and four children—Walter, baby Nora, and their Chinese foster sons, Dzau and John—they moved laboriously through the Union lines in biting winter winds. Less zealous adventurers would surely have awaited the advent of spring.[54]

More than once the lonely caravan was compelled to halt at some deserted shack for freezing days and nights on end. Back on the muddy byways the father and his boys often trudged for miles through muck so deep that even the oxen bogged down hopelessly. Sometimes it was necessary to unload the baggage and bear it on bleeding shoulders to higher ground. When spring finally dawned and soldiers of both armies at once began to cast calculating glances at the horse and buggy, William bartered them for hot meals in the chow line. Mary and Nora were then bedded down in the oxcart. After reaching the McClellan home they waited two years before passage to China could be arranged.[55]

While the Lambuths were preparing for landfall at Shanghai in November 1864, the Mississippi Conference met in Crystal Springs. Bishop Robert Paine, who had come by train from New Orleans,[56] gathered his decimated corps together and talked with them about the problems of war's aftermath. None doubted that hostilities were near an end. Lincoln's reelection, Sherman's march to the sea, and

Hood's retreat into Alabama were harbingers of dark days to come. Fewer chaplains were being called to active duty, while others were limping home along the lengthening line of retreat.[57]

Twelve preachers were still in uniform, and the bishop filled their posts with crippled men. They were joined by Henry Polk Lewis who had spent over two years working on his father's farm and preaching locally. During those trying months he had often gone to bed hungry like the seven others, including a black mother and child, in his care. He must have shouted when the bishop appointed him to a circuit with a comfortable parsonage and meager salary at Mount Carmel.[58]

Lewis' circuit was a new work near Prentiss which the bishop regarded as strategic for postwar missionary expansion. It was located near a railroad rather than a watercourse, for rail was emerging as the means of efficient economic transportation. For this reason Georgetown Circuit in the forks of the Pearl and the Strong was absorbed by Crystal Springs and Hazlehurst on the mainline of the Illinois Central. Farther south along the line, Brookhaven Circuit, including a mission to the blacks, was also created. In addition, new work was being undertaken along the Vicksburg-to-Meridian line, which had opened in 1860, with growing congregations at Forest, Lake and Newton.[59]

Five months after Bishop Paine sent his men riding into the piney woods armed with Bibles, General Lee rode into Appomattox Courthouse and surrendered his sword to General Grant, at least symbolically. But on that gloomy day nothing symbolical enhanced the realism with which Mississippi Methodists resolved to continue to wage the war that began in Heaven. With a material arsenal virtually void of weapons, they determined to fight for survival with sticks and stones and staves of the spirit. For currency, they were compelled to underwrite their enterprise with corn, sweet potatoes, rice, sugar cane, cattle, sheep, chickens and cloth laboriously woven by their women at the loom.[60]

Mistresses were not giggling girls awaiting the grand march of the Natchez ball or the square dance in the piney woods. They waited with a strange air of serenity for their barefooted men to stagger home to their battered doorways and dogtrots. To the eternal glory of General Lee, some of their husbands and brothers rode in on the mules which had drawn fieldpieces to the firing line. Now they would be able to harness their beasts to drag harrows across fallow fields. Lads who returned as men would now, to their amazement, find the hanging doors of burned-out schoolhouses open to admit them and Methodist teachers waiting to greet them.[61]

It was at the schoolhouse door that Mississippi Methodists set their sure course for passage across the turbulent seas of Reconstruction. Their native-born navigators, now virtually forgotten by history, included Harvey F. Johnson of Madison College, John C. and Almerin G. Miller of Centenary, Samuel D. Akin of Sharon, and George and Rachael Thompson of Whitworth. They were convinced that ignorance compounded by undisciplined passion had brought their romantic land to her knees. Now they resolved to press toward a distant commonwealth established on the moral foundation of human dignity and priceless worth of every race and creed of man.[62]

They began their cultural odyssey with the orphans of war, blacks as well as whites. Pastors and lay stewards were authorized and admonished to provide them with schools *gratis.* A conference committee unanimously mandated that classes be opened for freedmen, taught, where possible, by Southerners.[63] Yankee teachers, who flocked to the state in war's wake with their superior academic credentials, may have suspected a paternalistic ploy in this provision, but they knew little of this "different" land of romance and reality. Homegrown teachers who had learned their lessons on the end of a log could readily rule their own educational roost. Their determinate pride was soon to be subjected to the acid test of Reconstruction.[64]

Southern Methodist survivors of the armed conflict convened at New Orleans in May 1866. They were now confronted by the demands of postwar strategy. First on their agenda was the task of training a new generation of preachers for ministry in the "New South."[65] The small corps of men committed to "academic excellence" above and beyond the level of antebellum common schools and academies included William H. Watkins of Mississippi and David S. Doggett of Virginia. Both men envisioned the day when the level of theological education would exceed that currently offered by Randolph-Macon in Virginia, Trinity in North Carolina, Wofford in South Carolina, and Centenary.[66]

Assuming that an educated laity would eventually demand a ministry of professional stature, Doggett's group cited advances being accomplished by the Northern Church in her two theological seminaries.[67] "Oldtimers" cringed at the very idea, but in the end Doggett and Watkins persuaded the delegates to endorse the concept.[68]

Endorsement of a notion was one thing; structuring it was another thing. Bricks to build were broken and scattered in the rubble left lying across the fabled Bible Belt. People could only raise towers of Gothic dreams above the stately longleaf pines. But Wesleyans were a people blessed with the gift of "make do." Employing their pragmatic skills to the fullest, delegates to the conference decided that "biblical schools" should be attached to the existing colleges. This practical plan would not necessitate the erection of new buildings or the purchase of additional reference books for new libraries.[69]

The scheme was obviously makeshift. Moreover, it posed a threat to the colleges which were currently training young candidates for ministry in a new age. Finally, it would appear to disparage the "efficiency" of the old "College on Horseback" in which "oldtimers" had been so superbly trained.

Fully cognizant of these exceptions to the plan, Doggett returned to Virginia to plead his case before a Randolph-Macon convocation, and Watkins appeared before the commencement audience at Centenary in July following the General Conference. He went with the unmitigated blessing of the outgoing president, Harvey F. Johnson, who was totally convinced that "proper" theological education provided the most effective mode of reaching the hearts and minds of survivors of the late eye of the storm and the uncertain years of Reconstruction.[70]

But that was not to be the singular task of church institutions acting alone. Secular institutions of higher learning, notably the university at Oxford, were to play equally crucial roles in the cultural movements of the time. Thus at the beginning of Presidential Reconstruction the conference provided another of her clergy for the reconstituted faculty of the university: John J. Wheat, professor of Greek.[71] One of his students was a sixteen-year-old lad named Charles Betts Galloway, who entered the sophomore class in 1866 and was "elected as one of the junior orators."[72]

During a "union meeting" in the spring, supported by Presbyterians, Episcopalians and Methodists, young Galloway was quietly converted at a prayer meeting in the room of W. Calvin Wells, a dyed-in-the-wool Democrat and "unreconstructed rebel."[73] Galloway's conversion and admission on trial following his graduation in 1868 marked the opening of a new chapter in the history of Methodism in Mississippi and, indeed, the history of the commonwealth herself.[74]

As a romantic eleven-year-old piney woods youngster he once "sharpened a knife in length of a bayonet, and determined to carve in pieces any Yankee who dared to invade the soil of Mississippi." But this was precisely not the reason that it "is not an exaggeration" to "say that Bishop Galloway was the greatest man Mississippi ever produced."[75] Apart from the renown ascribed to him by his contemporaries and later historians, however, he merely epitomized untold numbers of statuesque Mississippi Methodists fashioned in the crucible of war and Reconstruction.

They rebuilt burned out churches with fervor becoming a frontier barn-raising. They encouraged and aided freedmen to build schools for their children. They were resolved that if Dixie were buried beneath a funereal pall, it was their mission to go about the business of resurrection.[76] They laid aside grievances against their Methodist Protestant brothers from whom they had been alienated since the 1830s,[77] for they now shared the humiliation suffered at the whims of the Yankee religious press. The New England Conference refused "to regard even a seeming recognition" of the Southern Church. "Shall we unite with the men who lead the great slaveholders' rebellion?" asked New York's *Christian Advocate and Journal.* "Take them to our bosoms, that they may wound us near the seat of life?"[78]

Pooling their moral forces to counter this unconscionable flurry of imprecations from the North, Mississippi Methodists and Methodist Protestants initiated a serious dialogue on the prospects for organic unification. The Protestants dispatched a memorial to this effect to the New Orleans sessions.[79] Although this hope was not realized until 1939, the exchanged overtures signified far more than friendly gestures. They indicated a mutual resolve to close ranks against the "avowed purpose" of Northern Methodists "to disintegrate and absorb our societies." If Bishop Matthew Simpson were to succeed in imposing his will upon the crippled congregations of Mississippi, then the two Wesleyan bodies would, for the sheer purpose of survival, stand together on the ramparts of resistance.[80]

Like Mississippians of every religious persuasion, however, dialoguing Methodists stumbled over a dominating problem in their own midst: the future role of the freedman in church and society.[81] The matter was exhaustively explored at New Orleans in 1866, when it was revealed that almost two out of three blacks had been lost to the Southern Church during the war.[82] Now the problem had been aggravated by the punitive provisions of the Black Code of Mississippi of the previous year, imposing a fine or imprisonment on black men who preached without a license by "some regularly organized church." In the face of this finite statute, it was the sobering consensus of the New Orleans gathering that the antebellum mode of mission to black men was outmoded.[83]

Their moral option was as clear as it was sad. With a "reluctance" that approached unanimity, they voted to grant independent ecclesiastical status to all freedmen, subject only to their wishes. When the Mississippi Conference met at Natchez in December 1867, Bishop Paine proceeded to set the proposed jurisdiction in motion. William G. Millsaps and Thomas Taylor were appointed superintendents *pro tempore* over four black districts—Brookhaven, Greenville, Madison, Yazoo—with a total of twenty-five charges served by five white and seven black preachers.[84]

During the next three years formal steps were taken to organize Mississippi freedmen into an annual conference. Highlighting the sessions at Vicksburg in November 1868 was the solemn ordination of five black deacons by Bishop Hubbard H. Kavanaugh. He then recommended that, in accordance with the provisions of the *Discipline* and guidelines presented by Millsaps, Taylor, and their black consultants, a legally constituted conference be formed. Governor Benjamin G. Humphreys, who had decried the provisions of the Black Code,[85] came over from Jackson to put the motion calling for the Colored Methodist Annual Conference to convene at Hazlehurst in January. His motion carried by a rising vote.[86]

"A considerable number of colored preachers" were present for the Hazlehurst sessions over which Bishop Kavanaugh presided. The new conference now embraced seven districts, twenty-five missions, and a corps of four black presiding elders, eight white and thirty-three black preachers.[87] In May 1870 the General Conference of the Church, South, formally authorized blacks to organize an independent General Conference of the Colored Methodist Episcopal Church in America. In December of that year the organizing convention convened in Jackson, Tennessee.[88] Mississippi's Black Code had been circumvented.

Five annual conferences from the southern states composed the nucleus of the new communion. She adopted the *Discipline* of the Church, South, as her rule of faith and practice, and presented William H. Miles and Richard H. Vanderhorst to receive the laying on of episcopal hands by Mississippi-born Robert Paine and Holland Nimmon McTyeire.[89]

Beginning in Mississippi, the will of black Methodists had been fulfilled. The will of white men was not imposed upon them. All-black churches originated in Philadelphia, Pennsylvania, half a century previously as a sanctuary against a Yankee storm of discrimination which beat upon their house of faith.[90]

79

Five: Rebuilders of the Battered Breastworks

The tumult and the shouting dies . . . On your own heads, in your own hands, the sin and the saving lies!
Rudyard Kipling

On February 26, 1870, five years of military rule over Mississippi ceased, and the state was restored to the Union. Although Congressional Reconstruction was still, for another five years, to be imposed upon this battered southern enclave, the Methodists and others determined to resist "the restoration of myopic secessionists to power."[1] In his inaugural address as governor in that same year, James Lusk Alcorn, a future convert to Methodism, denounced Secession as "a fallacy." The time had come to "go forward" to "the reconstruction of a government on the ruins of our own madness," he boldly concluded.[2]

Within three decades Theodore C. Link would be commissioned to design the striking architectual symbol of the state's rise from the ashes of war, the New Capitol.[3] During that interim the Methodists, unlike their biblical forefathers, Ezra and Nehemiah, resolved to rebuild their battered breastworks not with stone and mortar but with the moral materials of a New Creation etched on windswept Patmos.

The seventies and eighties were marked by revolutionary changes in the ethno-political climate of the state. A white majority in the bi-racial General Assembly elected a black Methodist preacher named Hiram Rhodes Revels to the Senate of the United States. He had worked with the Freedman's Bureau at Vicksburg during the war, and finally settled in Natchez as pastor of Zion Chapel where he emerged as a prominent educator and local politician.[4] His flock became such a hotbed of political activity that he and Bishop Vanderhorst appealed to the General Conference of the Colored Methodist Episcopal Church to proscribe the use of churches for political purposes. For enacting such a rule, blacks in the North labeled their Mississippi brothers as members of the "Old Slavery" Church.[5]

Nonetheless, Colored Methodists weathered the eye of this black Yankee storm. As the priceless gift of emancipation and Reconstruction, they outdistanced their white brethren in rebuilding a common life from the débris of war. By 1875 they were able to count a total of over eighty thousand members, four bishops, more than six hundred itinerant and almost as many local preachers, and thriving congregations with perhaps fifty thousand Sunday school students.[6] This striking postwar accomplishment by blacks had, whether for reasons of expediency or compassion, been initiated and fostered by white men of the Mississippi Conference.

Simultaneously with the creation of the Colored Methodist Conference, the same men also initiated steps to launch the North Mississippi Conference upon her way in 1870.[7] By that time, giving life to new annual conferences had become a tradition of the Mississippi Conference. Her geographic boundaries, which fifty-eight years earlier had embraced the vast expanses of the Old Southwest, were now confined to the lower half of the state including the capital city. She had never, since first setting Alabama apart forty years previously, been constrained to count the cost of lengthening the cords and strengthening the stakes of her Wesleyan Zion.[8]

Her latest gift to the household of faith extracted twenty-one pastoral charges and a like number of preachers from her safekeeping. Her losses were compensated by gains of nine preachers, ten pastoral charges, more than three thousand constituents, and such active local preachers as George Bancroft, Irvin

Roberts and J. M. Winbush. Although young Galloway, a member of the church in Canton, was lost to
North Mississippi, Joshua T. Heard of Mobile and
others were acquired in the exchanges.[9]

Contrary to lingering myths, Reconstruction was
not altogether void of blessings. For the Methodists
it was a time for learning the true meaning of aus-
terity. Only two station churches, called "high stee-
ples" by the circuit riders, were able to pay their
pastors as much as nine hundred dollars annually.
Most country preachers were compelled to provide
for their growing families on less than six hundred
dollars for a year's hard labor. Wilbur Fisk Glenn's
compensation consisted mainly of a scant two day's
supply of food. R. A. New, pastor and physician of
Rodney, was not only paid for both services in cabbages, but without money to buy a horse he simply
walked from six to sixteen miles to his appointments.[10] It was the Glenns and the News who
rebuilt the breastworks of the commonwealth long
before workmen could top off the New Capitol's finial with the golden "proud bird of Jove."

A surprisingly small number of "unreconstructed"
Methodists broke and ran after the state was
readmitted to the Union. Hervey Copeland, Richard
T. Hennington, Thomas L. Lacy and Levi Pearce
opted to migrate to Central America. "I have no desire to return to the so-called United States," said
Pearce.[11] But men and women of taller stature stayed
at home, having "long since learned to trust in God
and hope for better times." As a result of their per-
severance the troublous years between 1866 and
1874 proved to be a period of unprecedented growth
in church membership among both blacks and
whites. Never before had Methodist ministry in Mississippi been so replete with the spirit of renascence
as during those difficult years of Reconstruction.[12]

Statistics confirm the rhetoric. New missions were
established at Bethel in Lincoln County, Harrisville
in Simpson, Hickory in Newton, Pleasant Grove in

Kemper, Providence in Copiah, and Sageville in Lauderdale counties. In 1870 the Hortons, Scarboroughs, Russells, Eadys, Hammonds and Pearsons organized Conehatta Church near Newton. During that same year eight new charges were carved out of the Brandon District and five out of the Meridian District, and the Conehatta congregation grew from eighteen to seventy members. For the first time since the war the conference was able to overpay by $150 her assessment to the General Conference treasurer. They called this "coming out!"[13]

Lustily they sang from shaped-note Hymnals: "And are We yet Alive?" During the year more than one thousand whites were added to the seventeen thousand who were already secured in the sheepfold. More than one hundred and eighty Sunday schools involving one thousand teachers and other personnel with access to some eighteen thousand books and tracts were busy building mental, moral and spiritual foundations of a new commonwealth upon the ashes of war.[14]

Among the noted Sunday school superintendents was Colonel J. M. Wesson. After his Choctaw Mills burned to the ground during the war, this committed Methodist layman, much like Edward McGehee who had built "the factory" at Woodville in 1855,[15] rebuilt the Mississippi Mills at the crossroads settlement populated by two families. Within two years the population had increased to eight hundred, and Benjamin Jones moved into the burgeoning pasture. By 1868 a sizeable congregation and a flourishing Sunday school superintended by the colonel had been organized in the "factory church" which he built two years before North Mississippi was organized.[16]

Shortly afterward, another "colonel" named Henry S. McComb staked out a tract of land in the piney woods five miles north of Magnolia to build a roundhouse and shops for the New Orleans and

Great Northern Railroad.[17] Erastus R. Strickland, whose pithy axiom was to "put up suitable nests if you wish to collect the martins,"[18] was sent to minister to the influx of laborers. He "nested" his restless flock in the loft of a blacksmith shop before the generous Presbyterians offered their properly appointed facilities for preaching and Sunday school twice monthly. A Methodist Church was finally built in McComb during 1884.[19]

It was also a Wesleyan axiom that nestlings must be taught to fly. Erastus and other evangelists of the postwar era, prompt to exploit every missionary opportunity, were convinced that evangelism and education were inseparably intertwined in the accomplishment of the Lord's business. It was for this reason that he and Louise Judd had founded Wesleyan Female College in Jackson prior to war. Although the ambitious venture had been forced to close its doors in 1847 because of financial mismanagement,[20] motivation for the undertaking was identical with that which now graces the great seal of Duke University: *Eruditio et Religio*.[21]

The Mississippi Methodists were never recipients of a gift of eighty million dollars to raise a magnificent chapel tower in the heart of a classical quadrangle surrounded by a virgin stand of lofty pines. Yet neither were they unmindful of the fact that little Trinity College, upon whose foundation a great educational institution was to be built, had weathered the winds of war while her more prestigious neighbor at Chapel Hill was compelled to close her doors during the hostilities.[22] Inspired by courageous Trinitarians, postwar Mississippians dug deeper into the mud and clay to lay firmer cultural foundations upon which church and commonwealth were to build post-bellum institutions of government under God.

Resuming operations as a secondary school in the immediate postwar period, Centenary College began soon to evince her collegiate character. To augment the academic efforts of Charles Green Andrews and his faculty, John C. Keener, who was made a bishop in 1870, spearheaded a vigorous capital funds campaign for essential repairs, laboratory apparatus and books.[23] Enrollment peaked to its highest point since 1845. In their quest for proper academic training, young men called to ministry were provided financial support by a group of laymen calling themselves the Ministerial Education Association chaired by Thomas Reed of Fayette.[24]

Up at Brookhaven the Whitworth campus was alive with spring flowers. Young ladies were not to be excluded from their singular ministry. In 1871 the Master of Literature was conferred on ten seniors and the Master of Arts upon two. School patrons subscribed six thousand dollars for maintenance and to meet arrearages in Harvey F. Johnson's modest budget. One of his star pupils was Anna Clara Chrisman, who had enrolled in the music department in 1867 as a child of six. Later, as a young teacher, she volunteered for missionary work in Brazil, and was on her way to New York to board ship when she drowned in the Johnstown flood of 1889.[25]

Over at Meridian a citizen's committee, in a challenge to their Brookhaven friends, began building a school as a community enterprise. The pastor and congregation of Central Church offered them temporary quarters for the formal opening of "College Home" in 1871. A permanent facility was later erected on the corner of 23rd Avenue and 11th Street, and the name was changed to East Mississippi Female College. By the end of the first year enrollment had reached seventy, and the first class was graduated in 1874.[26] Shortly, most of them would become wives of yeomen and planters, politicians and preachers, and bear a new generation to shape the cultural course of the "New South."

Yet in the midst of this postwar cultural activism the preachers were not diverted from their purpose of enhancing their own unique cultural posture. Word was about that Commodore Cornelius Vanderbilt had endowed a new Methodist university at Nashville, Tennessee, to bear his name.[27] First among the graduate schools to be staffed was the Biblical Department under the deanship of systematic theologian Thomas Osgood Summers.[28] At long last, Mississippi could anticipate sending her aspiring candidates for ministry to an accredited theological seminary equal in academic stature to Yankee schools at Evanston, Boston and Madison.[29]

Indeed, it was expected that this Yankee-endowed institution of higher education would even surpass the level of "sanctified learning" for which Cambridge, New Haven and Princeton were so famous.[30] Centenarians should now be inspired to reach new heights of academic excellence.[31] Yet for young men truly called to the vineyard, but who were financially insecure or too academically deficient to try their vocational wings at Vanderbilt, obscure country schools in the piney woods would have to suffice. A "worthy" such school at Daleville, known as Cooper Institute, was operated by C. W. Barrier, offering free tuition and room and board for thirteen dollars monthly. One of his students, Mager Clayton Callaway, died before meeting his open note, and left his destitute wife, Celeste Lusk, to make good his obligation.[32]

Celeste may have remained at her husband's post and eked out a livelihood without abandoning her Sunday school class. Certainly, this would have been in keeping with the timely conviction that such schools were possibly "the most powerful agency in giving Christianity a permanence in the public mind." Considering the resilient state of society during the postwar period, it was seriously thought by many that this lowly educational enterprise could emerge as one of the more cohesive forces binding the divergent populace together. Clearly, declared Charles B. Galloway, "this is emphatically an age of

Sunday Schools."[33]

Youthful heads and hearts were priceless gifts, never to be lost in the wastelands of adversity, Galloway firmly insisted. "The cause of education was always on his heart." Shortly after leavetaking of the Oxford campus he married Harriet Willis of Vicksburg who shared his feelings and, like Celeste, volunteered as a teacher during their first appointment at Black Hawk. Although she was reared in a home of "greatest comfort," on pledging her troth to the young preacher she took an oath of virtual poverty. His annual salary at Black Hawk was a "munificent" three hundred dollars per annum, and it was for this paltry compensation that the young couple rode into the settlement on a January day of 1870 half-frozen to the bone.[34]

Yet he and his colleagues of every evangelical persuasion in Mississippi at the time were confident that "they will succeed who most thoroughly develop and promote the religious instruction of children." Some even went so far as to declare that Sunday schools had been more instrumental in converting the world to Christ than all of the accomplishments of the church during "the first ten centuries of the Christian era."[35] Citing the school at Edwards as an example, they pointed out that during its thirty-seven years of operation "only ten of its members had failed to join the church." They insisted that "our theories are right; our system is good. It remains for us only to labor, live and prosper in the prosecution of our aims."[36]

The realization of these aims depended largely upon the effective diffusion of religious books and other printed matter among the people. This practice had proven to be a highly efficient evangelical tool since the days of John and Charles Wesley.[37] For Mississippi Methodists to have looked "with indifference on this mighty agency of doing good" would have been myopic if not self-defeating. Dereliction of this sort would only invite the intrusion of inferior literature into the homes of the faithful, corrupt their children and lead ultimately to apostasies on a frightful scale.[38]

But, like the times, the day of the colporteur in a parson's round-breasted coat was rapidly changing. By the 1880s the task had become so demanding and burdensome for one man to handle that his preaching and pastoral ministry were losing their effectiveness. For this reason the General Conference shifted the responsibility to laypersons who promptly transformed their local churches into bookstores. With an initial outlay of twenty-five dollars they were suddenly in business—a very profitable business designed to produce profit-for-mission, not simply housekeeping expenditures.[39]

The Bible, of course, was the grandest missionary of all. With the creation of the state public school system in the 1840s, educational concerns at the grass roots had accelerated markedly.[40] Country people who had been unable to read, and blacks who had been denied the opportunity, were now afforded the privilege. But it appeared that the task of getting The Book to the people had become as demanding as getting the preacher to them. In order to counter this difficulty, the conference determined to place Bibles *gratis* in homes where none was to be found. One survey of five counties revealed that from "28 to 30 per cent" of the families lacked a copy of the Scriptures. Certain parishes in Louisiana revealed an even higher percentage of destitute homes—"a destitution of 68 per cent."[41]

The conference was alarmed at the moral consequences of this biblical poverty. She demanded that preachers and lay colporteurs load their buggies and wagons with Bibles and distribute them on their circuit rounds and business travels. Recipients were urged to bring their new book to revivals and camp meetings. Linus Parker, editor of the *New Orleans Christian Advocate*, made it "the order of the day."[42] As principal preacher at the annual Seashore Camp

Meeting near Biloxi in 1874 he and his assistants, John C. Keener, Enoch M. Marvin and Holland N. McTyeire, probably requested a show of hands holding The Book. Perhaps each of the sixty converts approached the mourner's bench clutching this holy treasure.[43]

Reading like chapters from Chronicles, the record of revivals rolled relentlessly onward through Reconstruction as if to remind Mississippians of the Great Revival which had swept across Virginia a century earlier.[44] Some two thousand attended the meeting at Holland's Campground in Jasper County, and near thirty-five hundred were targeted for "thunderbolts of truth" hurled at them by fifteen preachers at Hennington's Campground near Crystal Springs. The "happy throng" came by horseback, wagon, buggy, rail, and on foot, sleeping in tents pitched by the more affluent families and office seekers who often occupied "the stump."[45]

Campgrounds such as Seashore and Old Salem in Jackson County developed into permanent centers of evangelical and educational activity. They also provided politicians with a ready-made stump for canvassing. From the porch of his *Beauvoir* home Jefferson Davis probably monitored happenings at nearby Seashore. He was certainly acquainted with Keener and Parker, and probably knew of the oratorical gifts of Galloway, being himself a connoisseur of the proverbial southern art.[46]

Lest the joy of vacation salvation mar the Methodist vision of mission, visiting missionaries came annually to warn audiences that "respectable middle-class summer resorts" with only "a tinge of religion" could never win a "vast empire of darkness" like Africa or China to Christ. Those who enjoyed refreshing dips in the azure waters of Mississippi Sound after a morning spent studying the Acts of the Apostles would best profit from their example by giving a "minimum of twenty-five cents" each week for foreign missions. So moved by the appeal were the members of Crawford Street Church in Vicksburg that they underwrote a full-time foreign missionary in honor of the pastor, Galloway.[47]

The youthful members of his congregation banded together with youngsters from other churches and formed the Missionary Union endorsed by the conference. On the strength of their combined offerings, augmented by that of their parents and friends, Mary Lambuth was enabled to open two new schools in China enrolling some four hundred students.[48]

For Vicksburg's Methodist maids and matrons, Mary had become a true Mississippi heroine. Inspired by her example, they organized an auxiliary of the churchwide Woman's Missionary Society during the annual conference at Hazlehurst in 1878. The presiding officer, Juliana Hays, came from Baltimore to meet the preachers and install the first officers of the Mississippi auxiliary: Harriet Galloway, president; the Mesdames W. L. C. Hunnicutt, W. E. M. Linfield, R. S. Woodward; the Misses Annie DeMoss, Nannie Heard, Annie Linfield and Olive Watkins.[49]

Caricaturists made great sport of their "circles"— the gossip, character assassinations, tea served by "loyal darkies." But satire could not obviate the lingering fruits of their quiet impact upon social and moral forces binding the local community together, nor their leavening influence as champions of missionary enterprises at home and abroad. By the mid-eighties some forty senior and junior auxiliaries across the state, numbering more than eight hundred members, had been organized. Two of their junior members, Elizabeth Hughes and Carrie Steele, volunteered for foreign service. Funds for Laura Haygood's high school in China were doubly oversubscribed, and sufficient monies remained to support a full-time missionary and the Methodist college in Brazil.[50]

It was the son of their missionary heroine, Mary Lambuth, however, who most perfectly personified their image of "Medical Missionary." Walter Russell was sent home from China for schooling at Virgina's Emory and Henry College. After his baccalaureate in 1875 he continued his studies in theology and medicine at Vanderbilt, graduating at the head of his class in 1877. Having "never wavered from the idea of being a missionary," he was ordained an elder following graduation. With his wife, Daisy Kelley, at his side, he returned to China to walk in his father's footsteps—"one inexperienced missionary . . . setting his lancet and pill-box in array against a withering curse that threatened four hundred millions of people."[51]

During Walter's extended absence his "reconstructed" brethren back home moved through the "Gilded Age" with little of the fanfare usually associated with the period of prosperity extending from 1880 to the end of the century.[52] Compared with the "Robber Barons" of Boston, Philadelphia, New York and Chicago, few Mississippi planters, industrialists or bankers could have afforded membership in their exclusive clubs. The most affluent citizen in Tippah County was relatively poor.[53] Being men of means as well as Republicans, it may have been possible for Colonel J. M. Wesson and Reuben Webster Millsaps to have qualified for provisional membership in a Yankee fraternity.[54] But the chances were slim.

Even so, like the fabled "Bourbons," Mississippi Methodists could boast of their religious and political giants. They were moderates who abjured the "egocentric sectionalism" of the antebellum era, and they were not inclined "to inaugurate another rebellion." Their devotion to the past was no deterrent to their designs for the "New South." Their "calm dignity and splendid self-restraint" postured them against "the rash spirit of disunion" which, they resolved, would "never again be permitted to raise its ugly head."[55]

Between the administrations of James Lusk Alcorn in 1870 and the end of John Marshall Stone's second term in 1896, the "Bourbons," also called "Redeemers" and "Conservative-Democrats," designed and structured the commonwealth of the future.[56] Both governors were Methodists. Many of their colleagues in the three branches of government were fellow-churchmen. James D. Lynch, a mulatto Methodist missionary from Pennsylvania, served as secretary of state in Alcorn's administration. At his death in 1872 he was succeeded by Hiram R. Revels.[57] Robert Lowry, occupant of the Governor's Mansion from 1882 to 1890, was a steward in the Brandon Church.[58] The influence of this common religious faith upon the affairs of state cannot be lightly discounted.

Together with Edward C. Walthall, an Episcopalian, the "most influential Redeemers" were two Methodist senators: L. Q. C. Lamar and James Zebulon George.[59] After George had fallen victim of the yellow fever epidemic in 1897, the Mississippi Conference observed a day of mourning. The preachers praised him for not having departed this life like some romantic knight riding into limbo on a great white horse.[60] In matters political as well as religious neither he nor Lamar appealed to a vexillary standard of yesterday, but to one of higher moral and political excellence for tomorrow. It was not their task to "redeem" what by default had been lost forever in the eye of the storm. They were called to "rebuild" a new commonwealth solely from the débris of war.

In fact, few Methodists were inclined to call themselves "Redeemers." They preferred the more "worldly" designation, "Rebuilders." Builders were legion; The Redeemer was One and Holy. Morever, it was not their appointed task to build "a museum for mummies" adjoining the Old Capitol, but rather a social compact endowed with pragmatic tools to adapt to "the pressing needs and inevitable changes of the growing years."[61] Perhaps no individual in Mississippi more nearly personified the Methodist mentality which matured through the years of Reconstruction than Charles Betts Galloway.

On that cold January day in 1870, when he and Harriet had ridden into Black Hawk, the young couple had been warmed at the firesides of William P. Barton, William S. Chew and J. B. Streeter. The three suspected that a Wesleyan giant had come among them. Barton was a superannuated circuit rider; Chew and Streeter were active layman. Together with the congregation they were "captured" by the young preacher's sermon from John 5:39 admonishing them against searching the scriptures with such zeal as to blind them to the "Lord, and Giver of Life." During the year he "never preached an inferior or unimpressive sermon."[62]

Following fifteen years of seasoning in the field, he succeeded Linus Parker as editor of the *New Orleans Christian Advocate*. Although Galloway set immediately to write a biography of his friend, he also altered the editorial direction of the paper, particularly on social and racial issues. Parker maintained that "the hand of God" had sustained the institution of slavery, and that its good far exceeded its presumed evil. Furthermore, he had insisted that the pending civil rights bill of 1875 was designed "to Africanize our schools" and "insult and degrade the white people." The political "control of the Southern States," he argued, "should be in the hands of the white people."[63] This was precisely the position of agrarian Populists at the time Galloway assumed the editor's desk.[64]

Instinctively inclined to this identical posture since boyhood in the piney woods, Galloway wrestled with its moral implications until his death. Like Jacob of old, he never ceased to struggle with the angels. But his supremacist inclinations were rarely exposed to public view. He refused to write dogmatically about the Mind of God with reference to societal and racial ideologies. Neither would he presume to prophesy the ultimate consequences of emancipation, nor did he ever condone further discussion of who was "most responsible for American slavery." The surest counter to such inane exercises, he argued, was to do whatever was "best for them now." Freedmen must be allowed equal opportunity with every American citizen to fulfill in themselves "the highest purposes of an all-wise Providence."[65]

Like many of his Mississippi colleagues unknown to history, this man stood tall among the pines not because he was always sure of his mark, but rather because he fought to the finish against the beasts which sorely vexed his soul. It was for this priceless quality of mortal will that his catholic-spirited colleagues elevated him to the College of Bishops during the General Conference at Richmond, Virginia, in 1886.[66] His restrained critics called him a "boy bishop;" his vocal opponents challenged his moderate stand on Demon Rum.[67]

A long-standing rule in the *Methodist Discipline* imposed deposition upon any preacher convicted of distilling or vending spirituous liquors. The Southern Church amended the rule to include any member found guilty of drunkenness or drinking alcohol "unless in cases of necessity." The problem of booze had been bandied about in the Mississippi Conference since the days of Charles K. Marshall's crusade in antebellum times, but the first official conference commission appointed to deal with the issue was delayed until 1873.[68]

By that time the state legislature had enacted the "Pint Law," restricting liquor sales to specified locales only. Ardent prohibitionists decried the bill as a halfway measure. William L. Nugent, superintendent of a Sunday school in Jackson, organized a movement for statewide Prohibition to which Frances Willard and her "girls" lent heavy hands during 1881-1886.[69] Caught in the middle of the public imbroglio, and reluctant to challenge this action of a Democratic legislature, Galloway had come out in favor of a local option law.[70] Assuming that he had sold out to the liquor barons, and that he had pressured Governor Lowry into signing such a bill in 1886, hardliners seriously questioned his ability to fill the episcopal office. Yet Nugent was among the Mississippi delegates who placed his name in nomination at Richmond.[71]

Barely a year had passed before he was afforded a golden opportunity to justify the confidence they had placed in him. He challenged Jefferson Davis to a gentleman's duel in the press. The issue: Prohibition. The media: the Jackson *Clarion-Ledger* and the New Orleans *Times-Democrat* from August to December 1887. Davis opposed a pending constitutional amendment in Texas prohibiting the manufacture and sale of intoxicating beverages. Galloway vigorously defended the measure. After Texas drys had temporarily lost their fight, the President exclaimed: "O prohibition, sometimes called moral reform, what crimes are committed in thy name!"[72] The bishop regretted that "the great name of the most distinguished Mississippian should have been used in favor of the open saloon and against moral reform."[73]

Moral reform had emerged as a watchword among Methodists by the 1890s. As a pioneer in the movement the bishop contended that the "pitiless years of Reconstruction" had taught his people two compelling lessons. No longer could their church pose as apologist for wrongs "committed against the interests of the people," regardless of race, creed or social status. No man could be redeemed alone; more than an oldtime revival was demanded; social evils were the first concern of the church. This was the message coming loud and clear from the Biblical Department of Vanderbilt, and the bishop resolved that it would not fall on deaf ears, neither at home nor among the teeming multitudes in distant lands.[74]

His first official act as bishop was a visit to the Indian Mission Conference at Eufaula, Oklahoma. He assured his expatriated red constituents that after a half-century in "hell," they were not a forgotten people. Alexander Talley's disciples would continue to labor to ease their burden. "How triumphant we felt"! exclaimed one Choctaw preacher.[75]

Shortly, the son of southern provincialism set out upon a worldwide odyssey that read like entries in Marco Polo's log: Latin America, the Orient, the Middle East, Western Europe. That an obscure enclave of southern "racists" could dispatch such a man to proclaim salvation to the world amazed John R. Mott and leaders of the Student Volunteer Movement in the North and East. It also arrested the serious attention of proud Mississippians as a challenge to embrace the missionary enterprise as their very own.[76]

Yet northern "liberals," in their "partisan purblindedness," delighted in rapping the bishop's knuckles. How in good conscience, they asked, could he roam the world while a crop of racial dragon's teeth was being sown in his own backwoods yard? Were not the souls and bodies of black tenant farmers worth as much as those of Chinese coolies? "Equally so," he answered. Contrary to the critics in the North, his preachers were at his insistence taking a "more active and personal interest in work among the Negroes." Hoping to challenge more planters to duplicate the effort, on his return from overseas he dedicated a chapel on the Bee Lake plantation of Peter James, son of a pioneer circuit rider.[77] What, asked professional interracialists, who lambasted this flagrant act of "Uncle Tomism," did segregated chapels have to do with the black man's demand for civil rights?[78]

Removing his kid gloves to counter "extremists in both the North and the South," Galloway declared that the black man "must be guaranteed equal protection of the law." Race *per se* had "no place in courts of justice." A "white fiend is as much to be feared as a 'black brute.'" Lynching must cease. "Enforced ignorance" in inferior schools for black children was "illogical, un-American, and unChristian. It is possible in a despotism, but perilous in a republic," and "indefensible on any grounds of social or political wisdom." Repudiating the antebellum notion of the colonizationists that white Americans would best be served by removing the black man to the land of his ancestors, the bishop publicly declared that the African was "here to stay."[79]

Virtually every move the bishop made during his twenty-three-year episcopacy, every strategy he employed in carrying out his plans, was colored by this fact of life. Although he was no paragon of leadership perfection, having clay feet like every human being, he never lost his moral Wesleyan bearings. After his worldwide odyssey he clearly comprehended the fuller meaning of John Wesley's vision of "world parish." If on one occasion he declared that there would "never be any social mingling of the races," within three years he insisted that in a democratic society "the functions of citizenship are as sacred as the songs of Zion. The ballot is as holy as the Book of Common Prayer."[80]

He was visibly disturbed that Democrats who drafted the Constitution of 1890 inserted an ingenious provision designed to disfranchise the black man, an action he publicly denounced.[81] In the course of his overseas mission he was profoundly moved by what Professor Silver described as "the strange picture of one race disfranchising another to save itself from the consequences of its own vices."[82]

Unwilling to allow his people at home in their beleaguered racial enclave to continue feeding on their own guilt, he consciously co-opted the services of John Burruss Fearn, a physician, and Henry Gabriel Hawkins, an intellectual preacher, and sent them to China to assist Walter Russell Lambuth.[83]

His strategy was quite simple. It was meant to press the mind of his people beyond the confined dimensions of their own little painful corner of the world.

At the same time, he made strategic moves at home to enhance the dimensions of a more abundant and less guilt-ridden life among his spiritual charges. With the full support of the Mississippi and North Mississippi conferences he launched two strategic institutions upon their way: an orphanage and a new school. The orphanage was established near Water Valley, and later moved to Jackson across West Street from the W. L. Hemingway property.[84] The school was Millsaps College, located on that property dominating the horizon with its rolling meadows and magnolia groves.[85]

On February 14, 1889, the bishop convened a joint commission to proceed with plans for the new college at that "central and accessible point" in the state. Major Reuben Webster Millsaps provided the initial $50,000 required to launch the ambitious project. In April the Hemingway tract one mile north of the site of the proposed New Capitol was purchased, and white and black masons began laying brick to raise the walls of Old Main within sight of eroding Confederate breastworks.[86]

Six: Crusaders for Christ and Democracy

I judge it meet, right, and my bounden duty to declare, unto all that are willing to hear, the glad tidings of salvation.

John Wesley

More than one hundred eager white youth answered the first call of the school bell on the campus of Millsaps College in late September 1892. President William Belton Murrah's inaugural address was reported in the local press to have been "one of the finest" ever spoken "from a rostrum in the Capital City." In his audience were Major Millsaps, Mayor W. M. Henry, Congressman Charles E. Hooker, a faculty of four—Marvin C. Black, N. A. Pattillo, George C. Swearingen, W. L. Weber—and a goodly number of preachers and their parishioners.[1]

Even in an age described as the educational "watershed" of American history,[2] a college was "a thing of slow growth." Indeed, beginning with Cokesbury, more than one Methodist-related college had fallen by the wayside in the past. But Millsaps seemed to defy the rule. Not only did she weather the depression of 1893, but her purple pennants flew unusually high during the ensuing decades. In 1897 Webster Science Hall was dedicated, a row of "cottages" for needy ministerial students was built adjacent to the president's home, Edward Mayes organized a department of Law, and an observatory donated by Dan A. James, son of a circuit rider, was erected. The fall term of 1900 opened with six new faculty members and two hundred students, including a number of young preachers.[3]

Bishop Galloway formally dedicated the institution

on June 13, 1903. His discourse drew deeply from the wells of mythology which he had fathomed at the feet of John J. Wheat in Oxford. His greeting to friends of learning everywhere set the classical tone sustained by the college to this day: "This our first intellectual Olympia." The "supreme idea which called it into being" was *"to make this a pure college and not a university."* The administration was encouraged to maintain an "attitude to State education" that "should be forever friendly" as a "nursery of pure Christian patriotism" yielding "character and culture" to "meet the just expectations of a generous Providence."[4]

Ten days earlier the bishop had delivered the dedicatory address for the New Capitol. A throng of some twenty thousand stood in a downpour during the ceremoines, but the spirit of optimism abroad following the Spanish-American War left their spirits undampened.[5] Their hearts were warmed by the speaker's assuring words that "Mississippi was ordained by Providence" to occupy "a commanding position in the sisterhood of American commonwealths." She was not chosen to be last among the stars emblazoned upon the national banner!

Her role as appointed heir of "all the geographical and topographical conditions" created by Nature's God were to be devoted to building "a mental, commercial, and industrial empire." Her citizens were to cherish and nourish the "magnificent inheritance" of character bequeathed to them by their forefathers. In their rich veins flowed the "best blood of the world," and "by virtue of certain conditions it has been kept free from foreign mixture." Non-democratic "isms" simply did "not flourish in this region."[6]

The "stained and bare" corridors of the Old Capitol had long "felt the tread of giants." What Mississippian could ever forget Davis, the "uncrowned chief of an invisible republic of loving and loyal hearts;" or Seargent S. Prentiss, " a star of first magnitude;"[7] or Lamar, of "stainless character" and "dauntless leadership"? Each would have shared his laurels with honorable men and women of every race and creed who had sacrificed untold treasures just to stand unbowed before the storm to witness the symbol of their "beautiful land rise from ashes into affluence." Under God and the shadow of the wings of the "proud bird of Jove," they were now being rewarded fourfold for their labors done: this "triumph of architecture" consecrated to "the cause of pure democracy—to truth, liberty, justice, and righteousness."[8]

Surely, Galloway was not deceived by his own rhetoric. Justice was not always the fruit of liberty. Righteousness was not necessarily the child of truth. Affluence was irony to the presiding elder who had been paid $8.75 in the past three months, or preachers who subsisted on five hundred dollars a year.[9] The orator of the day knew perfectly well that not a few of his men might soon be seeking greener pastures or casting their lot with aggressive white agrarians resolved to liquidate their black competitors from the land.

Sitting near the podium from which he spoke were three men, one of whom would be elected governor within two months: Frank A. Critz and Edmund F. Noel were Methodists; James Kimble Vardaman was a Baptist.[10] The two Methodists were moderate progressives who stressed the high importance of education for blacks. Vardaman was running on a platform of unadulterated white supremacy, and apparently intimated that the bishop's opposition to racial "mixing" (miscegenation?) was in fact an endorsement of his position.[11]

For Vardaman's edification the bishop cited James Bryce's *American Commonwealth* to set the record straight. "Any policy which tends to inflame prejudice and widen the racial chasm," he declared, "postpones indefinitely the final triumphs of the

Son of Man among the sons of men." The black man "should have equal opportunities with every American citizen." If "the poor black man is never to have a brother, one or the other must move out. Enemies cannot live on adjoining lots without perpetual conflict."[12] Ten days later, on the all-white campus a mile away, he repeated the principle: "Let us make it possible for the poorest to drink of our spring."[13] Sixty years were to pass before the first black student was admitted to Millsaps College.

The bishop spent the last five years of his life building bridges between the races. So demanding was the labor that it finally extracted its fatal toll from his athletic frame. While chairing a meeting of the Board of Missions in Nashville on May 5, 1909, he collapsed and was brought home. He died seven days later. On the following day funeral services were conducted in the church soon to be named in his honor under the shadow of Jove's proud wings. One fiery editor called him "the most illustrious citizen whose name ever endowed and enriched the annals of our commonwealth."[14]

One year later Southern Methodists elected Murrah and Lambuth to succeed him. Lambuth returned to his China Mission. Murrah remained at home tending his flock, still threatened by racial discord and violence—still denying intellectually thirsty young blacks free access to springs of knowledge flowing unsequestered across the undulating green of the campus.

Yet he had laid firm physical foundations for his school beside the magnolia grove—buildings, endowment, faculty—with master mason's skill. His successors, David Carlisle Hull and Alexander Farrar Watkins, continued to build modest mansions of inquiry where young southern minds might learn to love the freedom that truth had brought them. Mundane materials like matching funds for the Carnegie Library provided by Major Millsaps and Isaac C. Enochs, a lumber industrialist and dedicated

Methodist layman, were forthcoming for one purpose alone: Truth. Edwin Mayes' law school was provided funds for one purpose alone: Justice. A chair of Bible was endowed for one purpose alone: Godliness. A gymnasium was built for one purpose alone: Strength.[15]

Stellar names began to appear on the faculty listing in the college bulletin. John Magruder Sullivan, a Centenary and Vanderbilt man, taught chemistry. A. Harvey Shannon, a student of Wilbur Fisk at Vanderbilt, taught Latin and Greek. A. A. Kern, professor of English, James Adolphus Moore, professor of mathematics, and his successor, E. Y. Burton, a Virginia man, all held earned doctorates. Men and women of tall academic stature seemed somehow mysteriously drawn to this provincial school of good learning, among whom were J. M. Burton, A. P. Hamilton, G. L. Harrell, G. W. Huddleston, D. M. Key, J. R. Lin, B. E. Mitchell, S. G. Noble, D. J. Savage and Robert Scott Ricketts.[16] Younger colleagues who later joined them included A. G. Sanders, Madame Coullet, Ross H. Moore, C. F. Nesbit.

The quiet impact of this collegium upon the mind of the rising generation of crusaders for Christ and democracy was profound and permanent. Among their students were young theologs of whom a new century would demand a new ministry. They had set their fathers' weathered saddlebags aside in the gallery of memorabilia and hung their longsuffering saddles in the shady dogtrot of the old homeplace. Henceforth, their *scholae prophetarum* were to be Centenary, Millsaps, Vanderbilt, and even little Montrose Training School. Caught by this spirit, one fledgling preacher led his cow twenty-two miles to Montrose, matriculated, and peddled milk to meet his school expenses.[17]

Governor Vardaman apparently feared that "high-priced ministers" like those being trained by Dean Tillett at Vanderbilt were becoming subversive to the interests of "the older agrarian values" and "the true spirit of Christianity." Much to the lament of Murrah, Sullivan and Inman W. Trotter, whose namesake was one of Tillett's "boys" at Vanderbilt, it appeared that the commodore's "munificent gift" to the church and the South might soon be lost. "Money power" would then, to the delight of Vardaman, no longer dominate Methodist ministry, and the College of Bishops would be free of control by Yankee "Robber Barons."[18] The liberalized voices of Vanderbilters who had "gone daft about culture" would then thankfully have been forever silenced.[19] By 1914 the fate of the university had been sealed by a power struggle for control between the trustees and the church hierarchy.

One year later the Supreme Court of Tennessee dissolved the concordat between the church and the university.[20] Murrah and his Tar Heel colleague, John Carlisle Kilgo, openly shared their "gloomy" feelings.[21] Now neither Millsaps nor Trinity would be able to send her bright young graduates to a "southern" school of the prophets. Methodism's "proud bird of Jove" had been swept from the finial of her hopes for a ministry equal to the challenges of the twentieth century in the heartland of the changing South.

Then, in the twinkling of an eye the old Wesleyan axiom about man's extremity being the Lord's opportunity became a reality. From Atlanta came a terse announcement that Asa W. Candler had endowed old Emory College with capital sufficient to the building of a great university upon the residue of ashes left by General Sherman's invading incendiaries.[22] Mississippi Methodists were overwhelmed with emotion. Good Wesleyan measure, pressed down, inevitably overflowed. Within months expansive Texans thundered the glad tidings that a small mesquite patch on the outskirts of Dallas had been staked out for a modest schoolhouse to be called Southern Methodist University.[23]

The "money power" so feared by Vardaman had

retained its stranglehold upon the church. But it was not the province of man, especially bishops like Holland McTyeire and Warren Akin Candler, to question the purposes of gifts from the hand of the Almighty. Religion and education, supported by commerce in railroads, soft drinks, cattle, cotton, oil and tobacco, would march "not two but one and inseparable" into the future.[24]

John W. Chisolm of Jackson was the first Mississippian to matriculate in Emory's School of Theology in the fall of 1914. During the next four years he was followed by M. F. Adams, J. B. Cain, J. L. Carter, J. H. Jolly and J. B. Stringer. With the discretion becoming his office, Bishop Murrah evinced his impartiality by sending Albea Godbold to Dallas in 1915. But no Mississippian was assigned to Dean Tillett's "educational derelict" at Nashville.[25] Methodist bishops were as adept at shunning as Amish lay preachers.

By that time war clouds were amassing over Western Europe. Placing implicit trust in President Wilson's proclamation of neutrality in August 1914, Mississippi Methodists went about their business. The conference celebrated her one hundredth birthday during 1913-1914 and resolved to present herself with a gift of ten thousand converts. "Methodism," quipped one witty layman from Port Gibson, "is still doing business in this territory, notwithstanding the presence of the boll weevil, charbon, hog cholera, and the Devil!"[26]

The bumper crop of new churches had never before been surpassed. The roster read like a market report: Biloxi, Capitol Street in Jackson, Clark's Chapel near Leaksville, Columbia, Fernwood, Fitlers, Forest, Gasqué, Gilmer, Greendale, Gulfport, Hiwanee, Moss Point, Mount Horeb, New Hebron, Pelahatchie, Picayune, Poplar Springs, Sumrall, Vicksburg, Walnut Grove. In the capital city the classical columns of Galloway Memorial Church were being hoisted into place to grace the facade of the

Methodist cathedral.[27] Down in Brookhaven substantial gifts from timber industrialists Thad and W. M. Lampton enabled the trustees to build the Mary B. Lampton Auditorium on the Whitworth campus.[28]

Up in Jackson eighty-year-old Major Millsaps deeded a six-story structure on Capitol Street to the college, to which he added paid-up insurance policies before his death on June 28, 1916. His contributions of over $600,000 across the years provided investment increments sufficient to build Murrah Hall on the ashes of Old Main which had burned in January 1914.[29] Preachers who were immersed in the romance of Methodist history prided themselves on having done what their pioneer ancestors had failed to do after Cokesbury College burned to the ground in 1795.[30]

Across West Street from Murrah Hall the Methodist Orphanage, which had been moved from Water Valley in 1907, was thriving. Physical facilities, including a power plant, dormitory, classroom complex and separate cottages, were being built at a rapid rate to accommodate W. M. Williams, his staff of twelve, and their two-hundred-member family. Benefactors included W. M. Lampton, J. S. Saxton, Luther Sexton and Isaac C. Enochs. In 1914 William Warnoch (Warnack?) and his wife deeded two hundred acres and a ten-room house northwest of the city as a home for older boys where they could engage in farming, dairying and mechanical work.[31]

Soon after the death of Bishop Galloway the Mississippi and North Mississippi conferences joined with Arkansas and Memphis in building a hospital in the City of Memphis. The Lucy Brinkley Annex was added in 1918.[32] Down on the coast the Seaman's Mission at Gulfport in charge of W. T. Griffin offered free bed, board, books and "spiritual conversion" for lonely seafaring men. For lonely young women from the farms Wesley Houses, staffed by deaconesses Myrtle M. Long and Alice Schreider, graduates of Scarritt College for Christian

Workers, served as secure hostels at Biloxi and Meridian underwritten by the Woman's Missionary Society.[33]

During the lull before the Great War erupted, Mississippi Methodists were obviously immersed in an educational, humanitarian and missionary enterprise of no mean dimensions.[34] In fact, their bureaucracies had proliferated with such seeming abandon that Bishop Candler,[35] brother of Asa, publicly lamented the activistic mania as a threat to "wholesome lives at home." The editor of the *New Orleans Christian Advocate* wondered just "what has become of the prayer meeting?"[36] J. W. Ramsey, pastor at New Augusta, was so swamped by directives from headquarters that he suggested an "Anti-Tuberculosis and Water-Works Day, Poor-Overburdened-Pastor Day and Preach-the-Gospel Day" with "a special sermon outline enclosed" be added to the list![37]

While young men in ill-fitting fatigues were engaged in squad drills to defy the Hun on Flanders Field, the poor pastor of Podunk was assiduously following orders from higher up to prepare his flock for a proper celebration of the Centennial of Methodist Missions.[38] Even a cursory count of the committees he was required to form, the collections he was instructed to receive, the number of converts he was to gather in, and the round of meetings crowded onto his calendar boggled the mind. Men's clubs, womens' societies, periodical clubs, fellowships of intercession, graded lessons from Nashville—they broke his back. If he "knuckled down" a "plum" appointment at conference would be the ample reward.[39]

"The Christian Crusade for Christ and World Democracy" would not tolerate "goldbrickers" and "draft-dodgers." If Mississippi boys were to die for democracy in the forests of France, the least their Methodist families back home could do was support the preparation of a corps of evangelists, teachers, doctors and nurses to heal the wounds of war around the world as well as at home. "The impossible must be attempted if we take the world for Christ!" exclaimed Walter Russell Lambuth. Responding to their hero's challenge, Mississippi Methodists laid an offering of one million dollars upon their altars in the piney woods missions and high-steepled churches in their towns and cities.[40]

On Easter Day following the declaration of war on the Central Powers in 1917, the Methodists sang "Onward, Christian Soldiers" from their shaped-note *Hymnal* (280) and began readying their moral forces to defend democracy. W. B. Hogg, pastor of the Laurel Church, was authorized by Governor Theodore Gilmore Bilbo to organize a company of infantry.[41] A unit of the Student Army Training Corps was established on the Millsaps campus, offering courses in French and telegraphy in cooperation with the faculty. Professors Burton, Hamilton, Mitchell and Noble volunteered for Y. M. C. A. war work. The Mississippi Conference endorsed the declaration of war and created a War Emergency Committee.[42] Pacifists were apparently blackballed by fraternities and shunned at daily chapel in Murrah Hall.

A procession of preachers jammed enlistment centers to volunteer as chaplains and foot soldiers. The governor predicted that they would be among the "first on the field of battle and the last to leave it."[43] William N. Thomas resigned his charge at Osyka to accept a commission as Navy chaplain. Clinton J. Busby, a local preacher from Hattiesburg, attended Chaplains School, was ordained deacon and elder on the same day and assigned to Camp Jackson, South Carolina. Elmer C. Gunn, Waights G. Henry, Roy H. Kleiser, A. J. Boyles, E. L. Alford, V. C. Clifford, J. B. Ellis and Linton L. Harger, who was killed in action on October 12, 1918, were among the first to serve as chaplains.[44]

William Fitzhugh Murrah was commissioned a captain of infantry. Inman W. Cooper, Jr., and his brother, Ellis B., were commissioned as officers in the Medical Corps and the line respectively. Alexander Farrar Watkins, Jr., and his brother, James Goulding, joined William Semmes Sullivan in Officers Candidate School. Enlistees in the 155th Infantry included Fred Dickens, George W. Dorsey, A. J. and W. K. Ferguson, Murdock Russell Jones and Martin Luther White. Michael Carter enlisted in the 140th Artillery, and Robert S. Sibley in the 331st.[45].

From other preachers' families came Navy recruits Hendrix Dawson, Mars Foreman, Irl Hendrix, Dan Warren Kelly, Richard Howard Peebles, James William Sells, and Gordon Lovelace Hunter, who died in Miami three days after Chaplain Harger was killed in action. Paul Greenway served as bandmaster, William Warren Huntley as a medical corpsman, and H. H. McDonald drove an ambulance. George Bell Sells won his wings in the Aviation Corps, and James William O'Neil was a proud Leatherneck. Joseph L. Greenway, Nolan B. Harmon, Jr., and Francis Stuart Harmon volunteered for Y. M. C. A. work.[46]

These preachers and the sons of preachers and teachers were among the fifty thousand Mississippians of every race and creed who served with honor and merited their combat decorations.[47] A current best seller hastily written by a patriotic preacher portrayed them as *Heroes All*.[48] But Lieutenant Fulton Thompson, son of Robert H., who had been "a distinguished member of the Constitutional Convention of 1890," was unimpressed by popular laurels ascribed to him and his men. "This war is simply making old men out of boys," he wrote his father from France. "I prayed like I never prayed before, and I believe the Lord saved me."[49]

This young officer would surely have saluted Bishop Lambuth for sharing the bunkers with the men of the 130th Field Artillery. Not even in the miseries of mission in China had he ministered to human beings "more approachable and open to truth than in this war." As a practical-minded bishop, he naturally dropped suggestions to sensitive youngsters that ministry might be their vocation in the postwar crusade for Christ and democracy. The church would be seeking such young men to fill the "depleted colleges and reenforce the attenuated lines of missionaries in foreign fields." But by the time the guns were silenced, Lambuth realized that the more compelling mission would be the volatile racial homefront in his native state.[50]

For the first time he had observed firsthand American blacks immersed in a social environment foreign to life in Mississippi. He was deeply troubled by what he saw and heard. Particularly pernicious were the pitfalls of "wine and women," gambling, and "the longshoremen and sailors' boarding-house keepers." Military regulations barring blacks from patronizing French houses of ill repute were all but void of teeth, and the bishop's insistent appeals to headquarters for assistance in protecting blacks from white entrepreneurs consistently fell on deaf ears. Only after he and his fellow chaplains cultivated the confidence of company commanders did headquarters staff begin "bending to the task."[51]

"Bending to the task" became the dominant theme of the bishop's frequent communications with his colleagues at home. Could the church do less? he asked. The "opportunity of the centuries is before us." Were the Methodists "alive to its demands and do we propose to meet it adequately? God help us. If we fail, ours will be a fearful condemnation as a Church."[52]

On his return to the states he continued to speak out in defense of the black man. He understood, far better than his homefront peers, that the social and psychological adjustments of black veterans to virtually unchanged agrarian mores would at best be difficult. When race riots erupted in 1919 during Bilbo's administration, Lambuth was "quick to take steps to prevent impending trouble." In the face of mob violence and the threat of lynching, he brought the full moral weight of his office to bear on the governor to restore law and order.[53]

Responding to the bishop's demand in a statement deploring violence and murder, Bilbo insisted that he was committed to enforcing the law "in an orderly way," meaning, of course, "within the context of a white society."[54] Refusing to be hoodwinked by the governor's "tricks," the bishop called a conference of prominent black leaders in Jackson to meet with him and a committee of concerned whites. Following a frank and open discussion of the problem, the bi-racial group concluded that "a generation had come on the scene" that "did not" and "could not, know each other." To forestall further alienation, if possible, an informal organization was formed "to bridge this chasm of silence and suspicion."[55]

The bishop was deeply disappointed that his church was too frequently reluctant to follow his lead onto the cutting edge of the perplexing problem of race in his state. From his experiences as a doughboy's confessor and surgeon, he had learned the meaning of a "new and larger relationship" which "must grow a larger and truer life" that would put away "minor things" and allow "the real values, ethically and spiritually," to emerge. God was "becoming more real, men are more brotherly, and Christ is being given more and more his rightful place in discussing moral questions and in vital faith."[56]

Although white supremacists among intimate friends and colleagues chided him for his moderate racial stance, they found it almost impossible to inveigh against his demonstrated ecumenical posture. For in the final analysis race was only one factor in the ecumenical impulse to fashion a new world that had been made "safe for democracy." It was ironical to Lambuth that his critics were at that moment engaged in a massive campaign of "Unity, Mission, Money" for the conversion of the races of men and for the fulfillment of Woodrow Wilson's vision of freedom and peace among the nations. Lambuth probably smiled on reading the entire issue of the *New Orleans Christian Advocate* on May 1, 1919, devoted to ecumenical world mission, or on seeing C. W. Cochran of Meridian contribute $700 toward the support of two young women who felt called to the mission field.[57]

If Cochran, the scion of a pioneer Mississippi family, is not mentioned in state histories, he represented the grass-roots character of the Methodists on the eve of the "Roaring Twenties." Undeterred by the aftershocks of war and the sudden economic slump into which the commonwealth was plunged following Bilbo's term in 1920, the bishop's flock was emerging from its romantically insular world.[58]

News of Bishop Lambuth's death at Yokohama on September 26, 1921, seemed to spur the homefolks to honor his memory in a vigorous crusade under the banner of the "Social Gospel."[59] By the time Bishop Murrah died four years later, Mississippi Methodists were beginning to accept certain realities about "brotherhood" from which they may have withdrawn in years past. In the language of the man whittlin' in his dogtrot or saying his prayers in the village church, Sunday sermons could no longer intercept hooded nightriders who burned crosses in a neighbor's front yard or lynched black war veterans who still wore their fading uniforms.

Yet northern preachers continued to identify Mississippi Methodist preachers and their people with these unconscionable acts of violence. That individual Methodists were party to these crimes against humanity could hardly be denied. That such brazen acts of violence were widespread and generally condoned is denied by the facts.

For one, compared with other sections of the United States the membership of the Ku Klux Klan in Mississippi was relatively small, and it seems reasonable to assume that the same finding applies to all the Methodist preachers and their constituencies.[60] For another, not a single official endorsement of the Klan is to be found in the *Mississippi Conference Journal*. Actually, in keeping with the joint pastoral letters of northern and southern bishops, the conference officially and specifically condemned the Klan and "mob murders in Mississippi."[61]

When conference convened at Hattiesburg in 1925 Bishop William N. Ainsworth assumed Murrah's familiar gavel. At the moment he was involved in high-level discussions with Northern Church leaders on pending plans for Methodist Unification. He feared that such a union might at that time severely jeopardize the tenuous racial posture of the Southern Church and result in further alienation between separated brethren.[62] Decrying violence and lynchings as "un-Christian, uncivilized, and subversive of law and order," he maintained that wisdom dictated that Methodists defer action on union until Mississippi had put her racial house in order. He then entertained a motion calling for the removal of "this foul blot" from "the escutcheon of our state."[63]

The wording of the resolution was almost identical with one recently adopted by the Mississippi Bar Association over which D. W. Harmon presided. It called on sheriffs to defend black prisoners "at the risk of their lives."[64] It was this prayer of state barristers that ignited the debate which one participant described as "a hot day in Court Street Church!"[65] At one point it appeared likely that the resolution would be lost and the conference hopelessly divided. That was the moment when Ainsworth vacated his chair and stepped into the breach.

He addressed the question in "strong terms," leaving no room for doubt that he endorsed the Bar Association's position. Appealing to precedent as well as moral principle, he cited the stand which for a decade the *New Orleans Christian Advocate* had assumed against Klan violence. He apparently quoted Alfred F. Smith, editor of the more widely read *Nashville Christian Advocate,* who prayed that no Mississippi Methodist had been among those who, since 1885, had lynched four hundred and twenty-five blacks.[66] The bishop could have reminded him that Washington County Methodists had only recently played a major role in the defeat of a pro-Klan candidate for sheriff.[67] When the question was called, the bishop's position prevailed.[68]

The "liberal boys" may have won a skirmish, but before adjournment the white troops of the supremacists would win the war. Waiting in the wings with a more formidable weapon than a sheriff's blackjack, they immediately interjected the name of the "Great Beast," Charles Darwin. His new theories of man's origins, they maintained, threatened to erode the "fair fabric" of "Christian Citizenship" in Mississippi, and jeopardize the orthodox posture of Methodist preachers. The doctrine of Evolution not only fostered the "criminal nature" especially in blacks, but exposed young preachers to the dominant influence of theological professors by whom "the evolutionary theory had been generally accepted."[69]

Apparently, the younger liberals decided to concede the issue for reasons of strategy. After all, man's origins were a *fait accompli;* racial conflict was subject to radical change. Conesquently, they let slide—as they had learned to do at Vanderbilt and Emory—a resolution requiring a law mandating Bible reading in all classes of the public schools "from the fifth grade up," and that books even mentioning the term "Evolution" be expurgated.[70] Midway through the administration of Henry L. Whitfield such a law was enacted.[71]

Preachers on Fifth Avenue were amused that redneck preachers and dirt farmers could sit and determine questions of man's origins in their segregated sanctuary down south. Little did high-steeple doctors of divinity know that Mississippi Methodists were engaged in prospering enterprises dedicated to the causes of human health, education and welfare that would have warmed John Wesley's heart.[72] "A new social consciousness," a "burning enthusiasm for humanity," had captured the Mississippi Mind.[73] William Sion Franklin Tatum endowed the Methodist Hospital in Hattiesburg with a gift of $100,000, reducing the cost of patient care to $4.39 *per diem*.[74] Substantial gifts to the orphanage in Jackson from Mrs. O. L. Biedenharn and her brothers, and Robert Estes Kennington, benefactor of Belhaven College, enabled the institution to emerge as the largest in the state.[75]

Across the street Millsaps was alive with boomtime activity under the presidency of soft-spoken David Martin Key, who had succeeded Alexander Farrar Watkins at the beginning of the decade. Physical structures that were in various stages of construction during the twenties included Sullivan-Harrell Science Building, Buie Gymnasium, Whitworth Hall, and Galloway and Burton dormitories to augment overcrowding in old Founders Hall. The Carnegie-Wilson Library was completed in 1925, and with a gift of $100,000 from the same W. S. F. Tatum who had endowed the hospital and a Baptist college in Hattiesburg, a Chair of Christian Education was created for the benefit of young preachers and women workers. In addition, the new "Millsaps-Whitworth System" was founded for purposes of cultural and academic exchanges.[76]

Then, unexpectedly, those gloomy autumn weeks of 1929 fell like a funereal pall over the fashionable churches of Fifth Avenue and quickly spread like a plague across the piney woods of the Magnolia State. Herbert Hoover became the overnight national scapegoat—a role partly imposed upon him by the American Methodist hierarchy. Methodist Democrats in Mississippi should have supported Alfred

Emanuel Smith, the "wet" Roman Catholic candidate. As ardent Prohibitionists they should have rallied behind Hoover, the "dry" Republican Quaker.[77] In the end, their dilemma was not solved by them, but rather for them.

In a landmark political decision never since duplicated in the history of American Methodism, the Church, South, "openly, and unequivocally" endorsed Hoover and resolved to defeat Smith.[78] Prior to Smith's nomination by the Democratic Convention at Houston in June 1928 the editor of the *New Orleans Christian Advocate*, feigning absolute neutrality, simply announced: "The wet and dry issue is clearly drawn between rival parties." At the same time Bishops Horace Mellard Du Bose and James Cannon, Jr., organized the Southland Committee of Safety as a protest against "the nomination by the Democratic party of a wet candidate for the Presidency."[79] The committee published a form for registered party members to complete and return as "A Protest." The bottom line read: "The Roman Catholic hierarchy maintains an insolent attitude toward the Protestant Church."[80]

The results of the election in the state graphically indicate that grass-roots Methodists assumed an "insolent attitude" toward their own hierarchy in matters political. Bilbo's slurs of Hoover's liberal racial posture enabled Smith to carry Mississippi by a margin of 124,539 to 26,344.[81] If Methodist voters had strictly adhered to the church line rather than the party line, the Democratic landslide would have been far less dramatic. The electors among their more than 100,000 constituents might, as Augustus B. Longstreet suggested in an antebellum "canvass," have swung Mississippi toward Hoover rather than Smith.

Mississippi Methodists had indeed emerged as a fact of political life. They had exercised the secret and sacred ballot to defy their spiritual fathers-in-God. They were "unreconstructed" crusaders for

Christ and Democrats.

But there must have been a more compelling reason why they adhered strictly to the party line than the issue of Prohibition or Smith's "Popish" connections. Perhaps the answer lay in their innate fear of a *Republican* candidate who would deliberately provoke their passions in a staged embrace of a delta black woman. As one Millsaps upperclassman put it in the autumn of 1931 while having his hair cut in the old wooden shack between Murrah Hall and Galloway Dorm: "When the Methodists go to church next Sunday at Galloway Memorial, they will pause before her stately columns, tip their derbys to 'Old Jove' all dressed in white robes, and enter the sanctuary to say their prayers!"[82]

This young man was presently to graduate and study theology at Emory under the tutelage of Andrew Sledd.[83] He was destined to be in the vanguard of a new generation of Mississippi Methodist preachers who repudiated Bishop Warren Akin Chandler's avowed segregationist posture clearly exposed to public view during the sessions of the Mississippi Conference between 1926 and 1928.[84] He was soon to pay the price for his role as a liberated crusader for Christ and democracy. He was to discover that his call to preach "the glad tidings of salvation" to "all that are willing to hear" was a perilous vocation.

Seven: Reconcilers of A People Under God

What troubles we have seen, what mighty conflicts past, Fightings without, and fears within, since we assembled last!

Charles Wesley

If any one theological theme dominated the preaching of Millsaps and Emory men from the Great Depression to *Brown vs. Board of Education*, 1929-1954,[1] it stemmed from Second Corinthians 5:18. Not a few Methodist congregations in Mississippi apparently chafed under the lean biblical fare Sunday after Sunday in their unsatiated hunger for the old-fashioned bread of personal salvation. Their ears were more acutely attuned to the rhythm of loaves and fishes than the drumbeat of Reconciliation. They were unable to forget those good old days when rows of Model-Ts, Maxwells, Reo Flying Clouds and one rich man's Packard had been parked in the shade of live oaks at New Prospect Campground.[2]

Now those glorious days and nights of shouting and rolling in the autumn leaves were gone forever. Dinners on the ground, quartets harmonizing Homer Rodeheaver's lilting tunes around the campfire, and the serenity of harvest moonlights were only memories. Mr. Hoover and the power brokers of Manhattan had left them ought save an epidemic of bank failures, foreclosures and bread lines such as had never been known in the darkest days of slavery. The Great Depression had become the Great Leveler. Past polarizations of "rich and poor, refined and rude, elite and common," had been dissipated.[3] The "forgotten man" now ruled his land with a scepter fashioned of crumbs which fell from the rich man's table.

On June 13, 1932, sagging telephone lines suddenly quickened to life with press releases from the Democratic Convention in Chicago announcing that Franklin Delano Roosevelt had been nominated for the presidency. "I pledge you, I pledge myself," he vowed before the world, "to a new deal for the American people." The "forgotten man" broke from the bread line and dashed toward his piney-woods home shouting Halleluiah![4]

The "forgotten man" had not been so overcome with euphoria one year earlier when Martin Sennett (Mike) Conner had moved into the Governor's Mansion vacated by the Bilbo family.[5] It mattered little to the common man that his lively Baptist hero was leaving office under a dark cloud of malfeasance tinted even livelier by an unfriendly press. For Bilbo had indeed been his friend and patron. He was less sure of the Yale-educated Methodist lawyer from Seminary who campaigned on a platform of "good government" and left no doubt that he was the sworn enemy of Roosevelt.[6]

Shortly after election day the Mississippi Conference convened at Columbia, attended by the new governor. Bishop Collins Denny led the congregation in the singing of the opening hymn: "Come, Holy Spirit . . . Look how we grovel here below." Like the state treasury, the coffers of the conference were also bare. So gloomy was the picture that only "the utmost economy" permitted the publication of a "materially reduced" number of copies of the journal of proceedings at a cost of $396.39. How under God was a budget of $646,840 to be raised? Certainly not by the freewill offerings of "forgotten" Methodist men and women.[7]

The conference *Journal* reads like a chapter from the Book of Lamentations. Mites were so scarce and attrition so bountiful that the conference was compelled to commit the unforgivable Methodist sin:

sharply "cut her askings" for the budget of the General Conference. If it was any consolation, the Baptists were in the same sinking boat. One of their convention secretaries exposed himself to possible censure for writing a stinging article on "How People May Be Led to Pay What They Promise."[8]

On receiving official notice that Mississippi was requesting the General Boards "to consider the advisability" of "reducing their askings," Nashville bureaucrats at first bemoaned this "act of nullification" by a rebellious people.[9] Then on reading the *nota bene*, tersely explaining that the conference was first cutting her own budget for missionary and social programs to the bone, empathetic officials responded with New-Year "Greetings." They would lend "heartiest cooperation" in relieving Mississippi of her commitment, and the bishops recommended that "special offerings" be designated for "thirty per cent" arrearages in the salaries of the preachers.[10]

This was simply wishful thinking at its episcopal worst. By the time conference met at Meridian in 1932 the situation had so worsened that the state was featured in a *Literary Digest* article entitled "One Fourth of a State Sold for Taxes."[11] Yet at that very moment the Sunday school-teaching governor was pressing for a sales tax. And with per capita income of $126 annually. And with cotton selling for 6.82¢ per pound![12] It was little wonder, then, that nonplused preachers reported that "income for this year has been considerably decreased," and "it seems now that we will not get as much as last year."[13]

One year later the misery deepened when the President proclaimed a banking holiday. Dismayed and desperate Mississippians, distrustful of all financial institutions, withheld their deposits and stuffed their cash into mattresses and began a round of vigorous bartering. Newspapers were exchanged for eggs, and preachers were paid in the strangest specie since the days of shinplasters: chickens, cabbages, cane syrup, collard greens, okra, watermelons, sorghum and over-ripened tomatoes.[14] Home-brew crocks were converted into sauerkraut kegs.

Rarely if ever before had Mississippi Methodists been so severely subjected to the testing of their moral mettle. But they refused to bend like reeds in the teeth of the winds of gloom and doom. They persevered in their Gospel of Reconciliation. In 1934 they resolved to meet their full share of the church's mission to the world. "No repudiation" of their "financial obligations either by an individual or the Church" would be tolerated. They would, in Bishop Lambuth's words, "bend to the task" of keeping "sacred" their credit. C. W. Crisler's resolution to this effect was adopted by "a standing vote" of the conference.[15]

"We're in the Fight!" exclaimed Professor John M. Sullivan. "A sound financial system" would be established in every congregation. Pastors would receive adequate compensation essential to their "efficiency, usefulness and happiness." Mr. Wesley's vision of world mission by a "worldly" church would not be dimmed by adversity at home. The "great task of quickening our people with a deeper consciousness of the Social Gospel" would not be forsaken. The social creed embraced by the *Discipline* of 1934, setting forth sixteen principles governing man's relation to his fellowman, would be the Methodist battle cry of "greater passion for social justice."[16]

"We must be unafraid and militant, but clear-visioned, Christlike," said the Millsaps scientist. The "lines of battle must be arranged and our plan of attack must be more carefully restudied." Evil forces— motion pictures, promiscuity, gambling, drunkenness, the "Charleston"—must come under the axe of legislation and the League of Decency. These old problems "with new aspects" must be fought with new weapons of the Wesleyan spirit in the hands of a reconciled people under God.[17]

Fred L. Applewhite of Wesson announced the declaration of war on New Dealers who had manipulated the repeal of the Volstead Act in 1933, labeling it a national disaster. The President had sold out his people to Demon Rum, "this age-long enemy so devoid of honesty, so inherently lawless, and so steeped in greed and crime." Society's only safeguard against it was "complete and external extermination."[18]

Yet this was only one of legions of demons to put underfoot. Inequities and injustices which threatened the integrity of the entire social structure must be eradicated. Methodists were duty-bound to perform deeds of social service which the crash programs of the New Deal Braintrusters would never accomplish with a massive bureaucracy. Pastors and people must rally to the support of the Conference Commission on Social Welfare which already had conducted mass meetings with an average attendance of three hundred. "There never has been a time that the people" were "as socially minded as they are at present."[19]

"Christianity Applied" and "the Gospel of Reconciliation" were double watchwords for Methodist mission in a new age, for the "fight" they were commissioned to wage shoulder-to-shoulder with other evangelical churches at the time.[20] The tide of liberalism flowing from the colleges and theological seminaries was leavening the mind of Mississippi's clerical leadership and spilling over into the domain of the laity. The racial impact of world war, the cultural adjustments of the Wilson era, and the Great Depression had created a compelling social climate of change which cultivated minds found difficult to set aside as a fleeting fad.[21]

But that possibility cannot be aimlessly discounted. A careful reading of Mississippi Conference records during the late thirties reveals a rather precipitous about-face. Resistance to the "Social Gospel" became more than aggressive; it became militant among crusaders for a return to the "Saving Gospel." The stirrings of economic recovery were partially responsible for the turnabout. The axiom of 1837, "As go the banks, so go the churches,"[22] began eclipsing the Corinthian letter as the most appropriate text for brighter days. If desperate times had motivated a high level of social consciousness, the prospects for return to good times tended to lower the plateau of concern for human welfare.

The threshold of economic hope rose perceptibly with the election of Hugh Lawson White as governor in 1935. Mike Conner had steadied the ship of state through turbulent seas, enabling the Columbia industrialist to take hold of a stable helm. White's reform program of "Balancing Agriculture with Industry" (B. A. W. I.) was a revolutionary concept enthusiastically embraced by the people of the Cotton Kingdom. It appeared that at long last the field syndrome, which had dominated the state's economic, cultural and political institutions for a century, was due for an abrupt alteration. The sons and daughters of tenant farmers, black as well as white, would soon be answering the call of the factory whistle.[23]

It appeared that "backward" Mississippi was finally on the move, and the Methodists joined in the parade. In one year "the collections on Benevolences" were thirty-four percent higher than those of the previous year. Memorial Mercy Home in New Orleans, a conference-sponsored care center for unwed mothers, was in "much better financial condition." The Woman's Auxiliary Society collected "more Octagon Coupons" than ever in years past.[24]

But, quipped the critics, soap wrappers could never redeem a fractured "racist" social order. Tokens would not buy bread for pellagra-stricken sharecroppers in the delta, nor for the proliferating families of black roustabouts laboring for long hours in the sweltering sun for poverty-level wages on river barges. Human rights and constitutional guarantees could not be purchased over the counters of Bible-Belt country stores. Not even a conflagration of coupons would be sufficient to burn down the wall of partition which segregated white souls from black souls in the Lord's House. That, exclaimed Bishop Candler, would be the day when God's people would be put "under the rule of Negro officials."[25]

Candler's portent of "evils imminent" was immediately picked up by certain liberal preachers and seminary professors, and converted into a convenient racist myth about southern preachers in general and Mississippians in particular. In the minds of some the myth persists to this day.[26]

The records of the conference—the published *Journal,* private correspondence, and even obscure manuscript minutes of quarterly and district conferences—tend to defy the myth. They reveal that while sharp and honest differences existed between laity and clergy, and between the clergy themselves, the Mississippi Conference was never torn apart on the issue of race. Although "smart alecs" in the pulpit were often "put in their place" by feedback from the pew, men like Applewhite, Crisler and Sullivan insisted that without liberally cultivated minds in the pulpit their church would ossify and die in the throes of the twentieth-century cultural revolution.[27]

Methodist histories tend to ignore the role of Mississippi preachers and laity as reconcilers between separated and segregated brethren in that restless era. Benjamin Franklin Jones, Henry Gabriel Hawkins, McKendree Marvin Black, Charles Franklin Emery, Nolan Bailey Harmon, Henry Ware Van Hook and Joseph Anderson Smith are names barely known beyond the conference borders. Yet they were among the larger cadre of clergy who forestalled a potential free-for-all over the issue of race and the Modernist-Fundamentalist controversy preceding the Uniting Conference in 1939.[28]

For instance, Smith was a graduate of old Meridian College, Drew Theological Seminary, and the University of California, later becoming professor of homiletics at Emory. He was a "liberal Evangelical" preacher, educator and missionary, and a "Christian gentleman of the first magnitude." He was a forceful adversary of white racists who through ignorance or superstition discriminated in any manner against their fellowman. His was one of the many unsung voices of that new "Other South" which projected the future course of United American Methodism.[29]

His passion for the restoration of unity among Methodists who, contrary to Wesleyan principles,[30] had been rent asunder for almost a century, was inspired by the ecumenical statures of Galloway and Lambuth. He was convinced that the opportune moment for return from this self-imposed captivity would arrive in 1938 during Methodism's worldwide celebration of John Wesley's Aldersgate "experience" in 1738. The bishops were planning a "Crusade" principally for money; he crusaded passionately for Unification to bring to modern Methodism the power and spirit of primitive Wesleyan life.[31]

After decades of aborted parleys a Plan of Union was finalized in 1934. Largely as a consequence of lay resistance, the Mississippi Conference withheld consent for three consecutive years. No persuasive power of their ecumenically-minded pastors seemed effective against their engrained fear of mandated racial "mixing" inherent in the plan. They feared for their local churches, for their public schools, their orphanages, their hospitals, Mercy Home.[32]

When conference convened in Court Street Church, Hattiesburg, in 1937, a distinct change of attitude toward the plan had surfaced. It may partially have been due to the general spirit of optimism emanating from confidence in Governor White's B. A. W. I. program, or to an informal discussion of lay delegates with Judge Paul B. Johnson, Sr., former congressman and a probable candidate to succeed

White. Nearby Main Street was the home church of the Johnson family, and the judge had several schoolmates from Millsaps among the delegates. For whatever reason, the plan was endorsed with this note appended: "Oppression, race hatred, and individual and corporate greed" had run their course among Mississippi Methodists.[33]

Boston's *Zion's Herald* never once mentioned this obscure manifesto of the Mississippi Conference. Nor did any northern paper note that the Mississippi delegation to the General Conference of the Southern Church at Birmingham in April 1938 was instructed to vote as a unit for the Plan of Union. Perhaps Easterners, who were prompt to anathematize Mississippi "racists," suspected that their brethren from the Deep South would best them in the final tabulation, which in fact happened. In 1936 the Northern Church had voted 470 to 83 for the plan; in 1938 the Southern Church voted 434 to 26 for the plan. "Blest Be the Tie that Binds," sang Southerners at Birmingham. "Everyone knows the Plan is segregation," lamented a black delegate of the Northern Church.[34]

One year later, Mississippi's delegates to the Uniting Conference in Kansas City, including Mrs. Paul Arrington,[35] were confident that their trust in the integrity of the United Methodist Church would be sustained. They were not disappointed. They were not precipitously thrown on the defensive by mass integration at every level of church life.[36] As called for by the plan, the black Jurisdictional Conference was forthwith created, much to the displeasure of such northern church leaders as Lewis O. Hartman who was later made a bishop.[37] But Bishop William T. Watkins assured Mississippians that they were entering "the portals of a new day."[38]

The bishop's rhetoric was at once optimistic and somber. While the People Called Methodists were busy uniting, the people of the world were being threatened by Hitler's lightning incursions into Poland, Finland, Scandanavia and the Low Countries of Western Europe. Although President Roosevelt insisted that "this nation will remain a neutral nation," fifteen months later he appointed William S. Knudsen to forge the resources of the Republic into "the great arsenal of democracy." By the time Japanese bombs fell on Oahu one year later, the farms and forests and factories of Mississippi were being transformed into a massive war machine.[39]

One year prior to Pearl Harbor, Professor Sullivan confidently asserted that the "positive answer to the World's despair" was found "in the Bible." Charles W. Crisler added that "the ideals of righteousness, unselfishness, service, and good will" were the sole defenses against "a world on fire."[40] Immediately following that "day of infamy" a year later he exclaimed: "International banditry can only be restrained by force." Brunnar M. Hunt offered a resolution during conference at Vicksburg expressing total support of the President "during the present war effort" and "the earnest longing for victory in this world conflict."[41]

The conference *Journal* makes no mention of debate, and Bishop J. Lloyd Decell, a native son, called for a standing vote. Not one man or woman remained seated. The pacifism which had "more deeply penetrated" American Methodism than "any other major denomination" was *passé* in Mississippi.[42] The Gospel of Reconciliation was indefinitely set aside by the patriot who was called "to bear arms and to offer his life" in "defense of his country, the finer moralities of life, and the sanctities of our holy Christianity."[43]

The land where magnolias once bloomed serenely in the merry month of May was abruptly transformed into a drab and dust-laden armed camp. Tranquil college campuses were converted into beehives of military activity, and lazy crossroads towns were contaminated with the fumes of gunpowder, gasoline and stale beer. Bootleggers, itinerant gamblers and camp followers plied their trades with reckless abandon. Confirmed cases of venereal diseases alarmed local physicians and military medics.[44] Bishop Watkins' portals were smudged with graffiti.

The more sophisticated civilians were avidly reading two bestsellers written by a patriotic preacher and published by Erdmans: H. A. Wood's *Victorious America* and *The Final Outcome of Hitler's Mad Dream*. Both books were recommended by Bishop Decell, and the ladies of Vicksburg apparently arranged for an autograph tea during conference in 1942.[45] Crumpled sheets of the Apostle's letter to the Corinthian Christians, over which Millsaps and Emory men had so laboriously pored, seemed to have been discarded like paper cups after the party was over.

By D-Day in Europe, June 6, 1944, the Mississippi Conference had sent some thirty chaplains to duty posts around the globe.[46] So urgent was the call for additional pastors to troops in the field, sailors in the farflung fleets and airmen in need of prayers to sustain their wings, that Bishop Decell convened a "Special Session" of the conference on February 27, 1945, "to attend to the election and ordination" of Wilkinson Baylis Alsworth and Randolph Stewart Smith for the chaplaincy.[47] This action was necessary because neither young man had fulfilled the disciplinary time requirements for ordination as elder, normally four years on trial. Deacons were not eligible for commissions as chaplains.

During the six months of global war which raged between the time of the special session and the regular session in Meridian's Central Church, October 24, 1945, victory had been achieved in Europe and 20,000 tons of trinitroluene had each fallen upon Hiroshima and Nagasaki. Among the casualties which made victory possible were forty-eight Millsaps men in whose memory the Christian Center stands today, towering above the tomb of the Major.[48] Yet, as T. E. Nicholson asked his brethren at

Meridian, would its spire serve as a beacon of reconciliation between the races of men, opening doors of "opportunity to reshape a shapeless world" in dimensions never envisioned by Tobias Gibson or Charles Betts Galloway?[49] Their successors had indeed "come to the Kingdom for such an hour as this." They would now lead "the exalted standard of an aggressive, positive peace following the truth of God" in a massive "Crusade for Christ." They would bring "the healing touch of Christ" to the races of men stricken with "misery and desolation."[50]

"And Are We Yet Alive?" they sang, until the rafters of Central Church in Meridian trembled with Resurrection Morn awesomeness. Bishop Decell said the "Day of March" had come. The "Crusade," initiated by the General Conference of 1944, was lauded from the podium to the gallery. Brunnar M. Hunt spoke for the presiding elders, Ben M. Stevens for the laity, and Mrs. W. F. Mahaffey for the women. Governor Thomas L. Bailey, a member of Central Church and intimate friend of his former pastor, the bishop, addressed the gathering. He challenged his brethren to close ranks, to win twelve thousand souls to Christ during the year, and to raise one million dollars in one year for the "Forward Movement," not for vainglory, not for numbers, not for dollars, but for a renewal of the "spirit of brotherhood, sympathetic understanding, and gracious helpfulness" among the races of men.[51]

The crusade was a stellar success. It was ongoing, reminiscent of frontier "protracted meetings." It sent the Mississippi delegates to Boston for the General Conference of 1948 armed with evidence of evangelical miracles which New England divines were reluctant to question. Yet many of them had probably never heard of this southern bishop who was blessed with "the heart of a warrior, and soul of a crusader," and who wore rimless glasses through which he could "see clearly" and "weigh carefully." Before his death in January 1946 he was "still tackling plans unfinished, tasks undone."[52]

One of the bishop's most admired colleagues was a local preacher named Charles Assaf, who had migrated from Syria and long served as a conference missionary. During the crusade he conducted five revival meetings, added one hundred and seven new souls to the church rolls, and recruited at least one young man whom he sent to Millsaps to study for the ministry.[53] If he was an unknown to Bostonians, they were reminded by J. Willard Leggett and other Mississippi delegates that it was the Assafs in the enclaves of the South who could "so transform men as to make the new atomic power" a "blessing instead of an instrument of destruction," and "save the world from atheistic Communism."[54]

Even as the Boston sessions were moving toward adjournment, ominous stirrings of Communist moves on the Korean Peninsula were featured in the local press. Spokesmen for the Mississippians warned their peers that "civilization faces the greatest crisis since the flood," and reminded them that primitive Methodism had evolved "the machinery" to meet the Communist threat head-on. Her only problem was that her misdirected zeal, not infrequently emanating from northern racial "do-gooders," was itself a threat to the very machinery she had created. The one thing needful was "a nation-wide, yea, a worldwide revival" of the Pentecostal spirit at the grass roots where the Assafs labored with silent but steadfast resolve.[55]

Tobias Gibson had been such a man, and the Mississippi and North Mississippi conferences were preparing to celebrate the Sesquicentennial of his lonely mission to "The Natchez." Under the guidance of their new bishop, Marvin A. Franklin, it was to be "the greatest year in our history," a "true revival of spiritual Christianity which shall revolutionize our thinking" and "manner of living." It was to be the Year of Reconciliation among the races of men in the commonwealth, the enlargement of "our missionary horizon," and the deepening of "our evangelistic fervor."[56] The columns of the *Mississippi Methodist Advocate*, which began publication in 1947 with some 28,000 subscribers, sparkled with glowing accounts of the numerous festivities.[57]

Bishop Franklin led off with a rousing sermon in the Washington Church on October 9, 1949, which was broadcast over "The Methodist Hour" originating in Atlanta and carried by local stations across the Southeastern States. During the three-day celebration directed by J. B. Cain and J. Allen Lindsey, Jr., fourteen prominent speakers, including Bishop Paul E. Martin of Arkansas, William L. Duren, author and editor from New Orleans, and William Warren Sweet, historian from the University of Chicago, dramatized the story of Wesleyan roots in the Old Southwest.[58] Perhaps never before had blacks and whites simultaneously heard the true story of their forefathers who had first joined hands around a primitive altar in a Baptist schoolhouse.

On the morning of the bishop's broadcast, similar services were attended by large crowds of both races at Kingston Church in Adams County, Jefferson Street Church in Natchez, Pearl River Church in Madison County, and at Port Gibson. Each was a landmark in the frontier history of Mississippi Methodism.[59] So great was the momentum of the festival that it carried over into 1950, when Alabamians and Mississippians dedicated Forkland Church in Greene County, Alabama, as a shrine commemorating the birthplace of James William Lambuth, the dedicated medical missionary to China. His son's spouse, "smiling, vivacious, black-eyed" Daisy, personified all that was precious to southern womanhood.[60]

Nostalgic as all of this may have appeared to critics and cynics, the fact remains that no previous celebration of Methodist history—1838, 1884, 1913, 1938—had so galvanized the People Called

Methodists in Mississippi. Never had they poured more of their moral and material resources into the task of strengthening their educational institutions, missionary enterprises and social service agencies. Never had more members been received into the church on profession of faith. Never had the spirit of reconciliation been more visible or vocal.[61] With the notable exception of radical racists, most of the preachers and committed laypersons in the conference had come to embrace the conviction that they were members of "an inclusive church. We intend to remain one."[62]

As Governor Bailey and Bishop Decell had maintained at the outset of the crusade, its ultimate objective was to translate the rhetorical "spirit of brotherhood" into reality. One of the more striking demonstrations of this resolution occurred in the governor's home church in 1945. The bishop, with what one of his loyal young Emory preachers described as "a foxy twinkle in his eye," invited Bishop Robert N. Brooks of New Orleans to address the conference in Central Church, Meridian. Speaking for the Central Jurisdiction, composed of black conferences in the South, Kansas and Nebraska,[63] the bishop pledged "the gratitude and cooperation of our Negro brethren in the Forward Movement."[64]

During the darkest days of the war two years previously, Charles W. Crisler had essentially pledged the same spirit of cooperation to the blacks: "the recognition of the Fatherhood of God and the universal brotherhood of man without respect to race, creed, or color."[65] But between the time of the Crisler statement and the address of Bishop Brooks, the Supreme Court of the United States declared white Democratic primaries in Mississippi unconstitutional.[66] Civil rights organizations immediately launched a voter registration drive across the state. Theodore G. Bilbo, "Prince of the Peckerwoods," led the resistance movement. In 1946 he won a seat in the U.S. Senate on the strength of his campaign promise "to use *any means* to keep the nigger away from the polls."[67] Intimidation of blacks seeking to register was widespread, and several deaths resulted from violence. For defending the rights of blacks, some attempts were made to "silence" white preachers.[68]

J. P. Stafford was a Methodist layman who apparently refused to join the resistance movement against the court decision and civil rights legislation proposed by President Truman. "Of grave concern," declared Stafford, "are the conflicts of our land and other lands in the area of race relations." Although the issue "must necessarily take into account the total historical background involved," rank-and-file Methodists should "steadfastly and persistently move toward the accomplishment of the ends which Christianity demands." United Methodism had "become in deed and in truth a world Church made up of constituents from all races and all countries." This was "an encouraging factor as we face the challenges of the future," he concluded.[69]

Not since the days of Secession had Mississippi Methodists been so painfully thrust onto the horns of a moral dilemma. It suddenly appeared that the spirit of unity and brotherhood evinced during the crusade might soon turn upon them as a dreaded nightmare.

Probably no Mississippi Methodist was more tormented by the seeming impasse than Governor Fielding L. Wright, Bailey's successor. Prior to his death in office on November 2, 1946, Bailey had sought to counter the mounting pressure from Washington in moves designed to elevate educational opportunities for young blacks. He had successfully pressed for the creation of Mississippi Vocational College for Negroes at Itta Bena.[70] Civil rights activists called it one more tactic to "fox the Feds" by providing a better-equipped school of peonage for black laborers in agriculture and industry.[71]

Wright chose a different political weapon in his

duel with the federal Goliath. A devout lifelong Methodist from Rolling Fork, he had been profoundly influenced by the moral stature of Bishop Galloway since his student days at Webb School in Bell Buckle, Tennessee, and his law school years at the University of Alabama.[72] Like his idol, he was a rock-ribbed Democrat. But when it became obvious to him that the national leadership of his party was determined to impugn the moral integrity of his state and violate her constitutional right to determine her own mode of extending the franchise, he bolted the party. In his inaugural he warned that "when national leaders attempt to change those principles for which the party stands, we intend to fight for its preservation with all means at our hands."[73] Shortly, he cast his political lot with the "Dixiecrats."[74]

Yet before making this painful decision he apparently sought the counsel of Bishop Franklin and possibly W. B. Selah, pastor of Galloway Memorial. The nature of their counsel is buried history, but he subsequently joined with Walter Sillers, speaker of the House of Representatives, and others in the defiant action.[75] Unlike the majority of newspapers in the state which endorsed his candidacy as vice-presidential running mate with South Carolina's Strom Thurmond—the notable exception being the Greenville *Delta-Democrat Times*—the *Mississippi Methodist Advocate* maintained a discreet silence during the heated campaign.[76] Perhaps out of loyalty to Galloway's memory and personal esteem for his Jackson pastor, Selah, Wright apparently never felt that his church had spurned him.

To his more intimate friends and fellow-churchmen, Fielding Wright was a quiet cultured Wesleyan moralist entrapped in a *cul de sac* of much larger dimensions than his own corner of history. Never was it said of him that he was censed with racist potions as "strong as horseradish" like Bilbo,[77] nor was he bent on denying the black man *"any"* educational opportunity like Vardaman.[78]

In a real sense, Governor Wright was a political reflection of the dilemma which by 1951 had entrapped his church. At that time northern church leaders were actively advocating the elimination of the Central Jurisdiction as a racist creation of the Uniting Conference aimed at smoothing southern feathers. The Mississippi Conference of that year adopted a memorial to the General Conference opposing what she believed to be an unconstitutional action.[79]

In his resolution to this effect, John W. Moore, pastor of Main Street Church, Hattiesburg, pointed out that Mississippi was simply seeking "a remedy for grievances" through proper ecclesiastical channels. He maintained that historic Methodism had never uncovered a biblical "blueprint for economic, political or social systems of any kind." Wesleyan tradition, he insisted, taught that men were "to deal with each other in love and charity as individuals, assaying to solve the problems of persons" rather than "the various systems under which they might live."[80]

Moreover, Mississippi was deeply concerned by the unwarranted activities of the Methodist Federation for Social Action dominated by the zealous Harry F. Ward. His office door appeared open to "any social, economic or political 'Ism'" which might drift by, and Mississippians wanted "Methodism's gadfly" put out of his pesky business.[81]

Among other repulsive activities, Ward's federation had unduly aroused northern passions to fight for the dissolution of the Central Jurisdiction. But Moore's memorial maintained that it had been constitutionally created for the very purpose for which Ward was determined to destroy it: to nurture and sustain a "leadership for its own people," and provide "a means satisfactory to Methodists of both races" to join hands "in the cause of Christ." It was for this reason that Mississippi had initially endorsed and supported the aims of the federation before it fell on evil times. The General Conference of 1952 confirmed Mississippi's position by rejecting proposed amendments that would have totally integrated blacks and whites in every annual conference throughout the church.[82]

Mississippians celebrated the triumph of their memorial as if it had been a second Sesquicentennial Crusade. But by 1956 the issue of race was surfacing with such compelling force that the Methodists finally adopted Amendment "IX," eliminating "all barriers based exclusively on racial and color distinctions."[83] The Central Jurisdiction was to be dissolved.[84] Under God, and under law, the Day of Reconciliation had hopefully dawned. One day, inevitably, Galloway's gavel would be handed over to the hand of a black bishop.

Eight: Strategists for the Ideological Wars

Be willing to know the whole truth, to see the whole character, however unpalatable the truth and however deformed the character.

Richard H. Rivers

Brown vs. Board of Education fell like twenty thousand tons of T. N. T. upon the Methodists in Mississippi.[1] Two years later the General Conference followed with a second bomb designed to strike a fatal blow at white racism and black racism in the land where Tobias Gibson had established the beachhead for an integrated church to be raised from the mud like an Ebenezer from desert stones. It seems ironical that the court decision on school integration and the adoption of Amendment "IX" should both have fallen upon the Magnolia State in the fragrant month of May. For in that month the state flower, selected by white, black, and Indian school children, blooms with annual niveous beauty.[2]

Few politicians and preachers had been tutored in their law schools and theological seminaries on strategy and tactics to wage the ideological wars to come. Bishop Collins Denny, the brilliant mentor in mental and moral philosophy at Vanderbilt, had employed one strategy: he simply refused to share a shepherd's crozier with a black brother.[3] Hugh Lawson White, then in his second term as governor, employed a distinctly different strategy: he brought black and white leaders together to discuss the probable impact of the court decision upon the populace. His strategy backfired. One respected black preacher reminded him that nine old white men had adjudicated the case. Politely adjourned, the participants of

141

the caucus went their separate ways.[4]

The records of the Mississippi Conference amply indicate that her members pursued a strategic course more in keeping with the governor's than their esteemed but intransigent bishop's. Between 1955 and 1958 the usual committee reports on Economic and Social Relations, which in past years had often polarized laity and clergy, moderates and conservatives, were not published in the conference *Journal*. Their exclusion was more than likely due to Bishop Franklin's avowed determination to maintain at least a semblance of Christian "balance" among his people who were faced with the rising tide of public resistance to the mandate of the Warren Court,[5] compounded by their displeasure with actions of the General Conference.

Both the governor and the bishop, however limply, exerted every effort to pour oil on the restless waters roughed by torrents of editorials punctuating the pages of weeklies and dailies across the state. In the attempt to inject a note of sanity into the open imbroglio, Robert L. Ezelle offered a carefully conceived resolution before the conference of 1955 convened in Galloway Memorial Church.

First, he explained that he was acting as spokesman for the Board of Education rather than the Committee on Economic and Social Relations. He then quoted passages from editorials in the secular press and the *Mississippi Methodist Advocate* which had appeared before and after the court decision of the previous year. From the *Advocate* he quoted an editorial warning that "this segregation issue will become increasingly serious and in many areas it will be accompanied by distressing consequences." The Methodists were "not to decide whether segregation or integration shall be the policy of public education in the South or anywhere else." Yet with "white institutions open to them, Negroes will have a wider range of schools to choose from," thus enhancing their opportunities for increased educational efficiency.⁶

For having suggested this academic "mixing," the editor had been slandered by "many people in the Jackson area" for virtually endorsing "the Supreme Court decision and integration." Then in his own words Ezelle congratulated these same critics for "what is already being done" to educate a black leadership, but "we should do more to help in this great cause." He next offered his resolution that a joint committee of the Mississippi and North Mississippi conferences study the immediate needs of Rust College in Holly Springs and "other church related institutions where Negro leadership is trained." His motion was adopted without debate.⁷

Robert Ezelle was not a cunning man, but his presentation was strategically flawless. Not once in his own words did he even allude to segregation, integration, separate but equal, all possible haste, or Thurgood Marshall's role as counsel for the N. A. A. C. P. in the court decision.⁸ He had painlessly placed his conference on record as patron of schools for black sons and daughters wherever Methodist influence could be brought to bear. The effect of his strategy was measured silence—a silence that was sustained until conference met at Gulfport in 1959.⁹

It was there, near *Beauvoir* and Seashore Campground, that the citadel of Southern Methodism was declared under siege on two of her exposed flanks. The Yankee apostles of integration had violated the sanctity of their covenant with Mississippi by threatening to impose black rule over them. The Democratic politicians ruling their own state threatened to impose upon their preachers a morally unconscionable reign of white-supremacist segregationism which would both defy and destroy their sacred calling to proclaim the Gospel to Jew and Gentile, bond and free, white and black.

For the first time in five years a last-minute report from the Committee on Economic and Social Relations was submitted to the conference by John H.

Morrow, Jr., chairman. A "deplorable situation" demanded "immediate attention," declared the Emory graduate in a 1,350-word landmine padded with soporifics.[10] The "use of the racial situation and racial prejudice by politicians" to round up votes was a travesty on democratic principles. The time had come for "sober-minded and responsible citizens" to be elected to public office "and the radicals bypassed." Since 1956 Governor James Plemon Coleman had preached the doctrine of "cool thinking on racial problems," but now his choice of a successor, Carroll Gartin, was being challenged by an alleged racist, Ross Barnett. Election day was less than six months away.[11]

Discreetly omitting names, the manifesto was an unyielding call for Mississippi Methodists to recapture and exert the political expertise for which they were famous during the days of Bishop Asbury[12] and the evangelicals of Oxford and Cambridge in Wesley's time. They had been zealous political activists and advocates of social change, and any candidate in Mississippi known for his "adamant opposition" to such societal changes in public school education and race relations deserved the stern challenge of Methodist electors.[13]

Among Morrow's listeners were clergy and laity who would undoubtedly cast their ballots for Barnett in November. A few, perhaps, were active members of the all-white Citizens' Council, organized in 1954 to resist "implementation of the Court's decision." As "the almost unchallenged arbiter of Mississippi politics,"[14] the council was backing the Baptist Sunday-school teacher's candidacy to the hilt. The same was true of prominent leaders in the Independent Methodist Church which had defected from the Mississippi Conference after the court's decision.[15] They were to enjoy "apparently limitless access" to Barnett's office during the next four years.[16]

When conference convened in Galloway Memorial

on June 14, 1960, news reporters were much in evidence. Morrow's manifesto had sharply polarized the Methodists, and a well-orchestrated open forum on the racial policy of The United Church had been announced to the media. Panelists were W. D. Myers, J. C. Satterfield, J. P. Stafford and B. M. Stevens. The subject to be discussed was a resolution recently adopted by the church-sponsored Conference on Human Relations at Dallas calling for "a genuine interracial experience by the association" of blacks and whites in their churches and schools.[17]

Up to this point Mississippi Methodists had pursued a moderate course on the issue of school integration. Unlike other denominations in the state, they had refused to panic and stampede in the hurried formation of all-white academies. But the Dallas proposal broke their patient backs. Advocating "prompt and reasonable" integration of public schools was one thing; the demand for integration of every church congregation and institution was quite another thing. It was this ideological dichotomy, raised but not resolved by the panelists in 1960, that was to dominate the Mississippi Methodist Mind during the troubled decade in which one legislator vowed "to abolish The Methodist Church in Mississippi."[18]

The reason for this outburst was obvious. Franklin and his successor, Edward J. Pendergrass, refused to bow to pressures brought by the Citizens' Council and other zealots of the "resistance movement." The two bishops, deeming it a "sacred responsibility" to "build bridges" between the races, ignored motions condemning the action of the Dallas conference.[19] Supported by Ezelle, Nat Rogers and H. Ellis Finger, president of Millsaps since 1955, they demonstrated uncanny adherence to Wesleyan principles during Barnett's administration, 1960-1964.[20] In the face of widespread demonstrations they never seemed to waver far from their ultimate goal of building bridges such as Governor White accomplished in the field of "better educational opportunities" for young blacks with the aid of the legislature's Legal Advisory Committee in 1954.[21]

But the record reveals that Methodists were doing little in behalf of "equalization" efforts. "In this regard," it was pointed out, they had left undone what "we should have done." Only eighty-six of their 308 congregations had sent in offerings for Rust College, and of that number only thirteen had organized a local Committee on Race Relations mandated by the conference.[22]

Before Barnett and Franklin had completed their respective terms in 1964, saccharine ecclesiastical pronouncements and clever legislative enactments were consumed like scraps of paper in the fires of a "Reign of Terror" which engulfed the state.[23] Bland statements by the conference deploring the activities of demonstrators and praising blacks for "not participating in, or promoting, such demonstrations," failed to deter "Freedom Riders" from their appointed rounds, or "outsiders" recruited by the N.A.A.C.P., C.O.R.E. and S.N.C.C. from swarming over the farmlands and magnolia groves like locusts over Egypt. The "Long hot Summer" in McComb, Philadelphia, Biloxi, Hattiesburg, Clarksdale and at Tougaloo College left a residue of pent-up passions to await the whirlwind.[24]

During 1962 responsible reporters who had also swarmed upon the beleaguered enclave began to sense that "exciting circuses" in "redneck country" were of graver import than their distant publishers suspected. They realized that moral and constitutional principles for which a war had been fought one century ago were once again being tried in the fire along the village streets of Mississippi and on the campus of the university.[25] In June following James Meredith's federally enforced admission to Ole Miss, Medgar Evers was felled by a sniper's bullet in his own driveway.[26] On June 21, 1964, three young student "radicals" from the East—James Chaney, Andrew Goodman and Michael Schwerner—were murdered and buried in an earthern dam bulldozed from Choctaw happy-hunting grounds lost in limbo.[27]

By this time sensitive Methodists had awakened to the fact that a "balanced" course *per se* was as dangerous as it was deceptive. They were now convinced that strategies concocted in smoke-filled rooms of the Capitol or smokeless anterooms of some local sanctuary were no more able to quench the conflagration than the tissue on which high-sounding resolutions were written. Their church and their commonwealth were entrapped in ideological conflict which neither the Civil Rights Act of 1964 nor the Voting Rights Act of 1965 could contain or resolve. They were as morally incapable of assuming a passive posture in the face of this threat as their forebears were in escaping "the ravages of yellow fever by hiding in the woods."[28]

Not even the military might of the United States Government displayed "after church" in Oxford on Sunday, September 30, 1962, had been able to extinguish the flaming torch of what the editor of the *Mississippi Methodist Advocate* called "the 'new day' " being "ushered in."[29] And that "new day," he added poignantly, would demand personal sacrifices of men who walked tall bearing their burden into the future—men like those giants who emerged from the First Reconstruction to rebuild the commonwealth with broken bricks kiln-dried in the fires of adversity.

When conference gathered for her somber session in 1962 David Holcomb McKeithen and Reuben Inman Moore, Jr., both Emory men, presented their report on Social and Economic Relations. It was yet another 20,000-ton bomb, stripped of jargon, and precisely on target: No tax funds shall hereafter be diverted to "any organization" for "the promotion of partisan viewpoints."[30] Methodists would no longer stand idly by while the governor funneled the peoples' money into a radio and television show called "Forum" sponsored by the Citizens' Council through the "good offices" of the tax-supported State Sovereignty Commission. Before the show was terminated a year later, some $193,000 of taxpayers' money had been pumped into the media project.[31]

Everyone understood that the manipulation of tax funds for pet projects was an established practice in Mississippi. But this was not the point of the report presented by the McKeithen committee. It aimed at a much more disturbing threat to the church herself.

While the Sovereignty Commission was pouring money into "Forum," it was also accumulating an extensive portfolio on "radicals," including certain "liberal" Methodist preachers who had "gone away to school" at Atlanta, or Durham, or Dallas, or New Haven, and returned home with half their brains pushed "out of their skulls" by "edication." Moore suspected that he was on the "hit list," and he dreaded the thought that soon the twenty-three young men studying for their degree in divinity would, on their return home, be prime targets of the Sovereignty Commission.[32]

But Moore and twenty-seven other "young Turks" were not about to relegate the report to the lifeless pages of the conference *Journal*. On January 3, 1963, the *Mississippi Methodist Advocate* published their eye-opening statement of "Conviction." They had now learned from their study of church history what Martin Luther meant when he allegedly declared before the Diet of Worms in 1721: "Here I stand. I can do no other"! Three months after their "Born of Conviction" declaration was symbolically posted on the oaken doors of Galloway Memorial, decrying racial segregation and discrimination, Moore "removed" to the Southern California-Arizona Conference, and six of his colleagues "departed" their native state in that same year.[33]

The "Mississippi Seven of '63" were only a remnant of seminary men who had wiped Mississippi mud from their feet since 1954. So distraught was Bishop Franklin that he co-opted a special investigating committee, chaired by John Speed, to probe the root cause of the exodus. Before Speed and his pollsters could collate their findings and report to conference, twenty-two other seminary trained preachers had joined the exodus. With one exception, all transferred to eastern, northern or western conferences. The final draft of the report, based on forty-five replies to questionnaires mailed to seminary graduates who had taken leave of the conference in the past five years, was almost uniformly void of rancor.

Only one man moved for a "higher salary." He was at least candid! Several replied that "larger opportunities for service elsewhere" were too challenging to resist. This was a familiar Methodist melody. The "segregation-integration question" was surprisingly downplayed. "Dissatisfaction with conference leadership" and "conference politics" elicited the most straightforward replies. The conference was too entirely "controlled by one faction," and appointments depended solely on how one played the game.[34]

Professional ethics prevented positive identification of the kingmaker or makers. But following the change in command and the agonizing readjustments which naturally ensued, two simple results began to emerge: First, "today the church is stronger than ever." Second, "there can be no color bar in a Christian church."[35] Perhaps it was inevitable if not providential that this *consensus gentium* should have been shaped in the cathedral church of Mississippi Methodism. For, as the pastor who lived through the racial passiontide between 1963 and 1966 affirmed in 1980: "One sees today a Galloway walking in health and strength."[36]

G. Ross Freeman was guest preacher for conference in Galloway Memorial, May 28-31, 1963. Bishop Franklin and the pastor, W. B. Selah, warned the Emory professor that the doors of the church might be closed to blacks over their official protest. Divesting himself of his doctor's gown and donning the prophet's mantle, the teacher of the teachers of God preached from Matthew 10:16-18. He warned that in a society teeming with wolves shrouded in white sheets "we must be wise and outthink the pagan," be "sensitive to the currents around us, to the issues that effect mankind," to "the things that are taking place in the earth." Yet, he concluded, "in the time of greatest need, the Church has Laryngitis."[37]

Methodist circuit riders had made full use of this hermeneutic tactic since pioneer times. Freeman knew well that his protégés were free of throat trouble. He knew that the real problem was a cacophony of strident voices reminiscent of those which had crumbled ancient Babel. He knew that the only Mississippian ever elected president of the American Bar Association and a leading member of Selah's congregation had recently published an erudite challenge to the Civil Rights Act of 1964.[38] He knew that the editor of the *Mississippi Methodist Advocate* had chastised those who closed church doors to "international guests." Such actions, he added, made "explanations impossible and apologies by concerned Christians extremely difficult."[39]

Two weeks following the adjournment of conference, Bishop Franklin, weary of the warfare which was devastating his household, announced his retirement at the next annual meeting. For sixteen years he had led his people through times of celebration, crisis, change. A 5,000-word in-depth study of his episcopate revealed that much had been accomplished, much was to be lamented, much was yet to be undertaken by his successors, beginning with Edward J. Pendergrass.[40]

One of the new bishop's first acts was to call at the Governor's Mansion. It was motivated by reasons other than courtesy or pastoral duty, although Paul

B. Johnson, Jr., and his family were staunch Methodists. Having read press accounts of the governor's inaugural of January 21, Pendergrass determined to seek out this man who had vowed that "hate, prejudice, and ignorance" would no longer dominate the life of the Magnolia State.[41]

As responsible leaders who shared the burdens common to church and state, and who saw eye-to-eye on many vital issues, the two men apparently became fast friends. Not since the administration of Fielding L. Wright had a Methodist bishop enjoyed such an intimate pastoral liaison with a governor, and it is not unthinkable that their ideological strategies as joint chiefs of staff measurably determined the direction their respective constituents would pursue during the foreseeable future.

One very visible indication of their joint strategy occurred during conference at Galloway in June 1965. Possibly setting aside the caution of the new pastor, W. J. Cunningham, the bishop arranged for the governor to address an overflow audience in the church on Sunday evening, the fifth.[42] Cunningham apparently entertained serious misgivings about Johnson's recent and much-publicized stand with Barnett before the Ole Miss school door when Meredith knocked for admission. In any event, relations between the *pastor pastorum* and his controversial cardinal pastor began a chilling process that consummated in Cunningham's resignation at the next annual conference. In the end he could conscientiously claim "I helped open the doors" of the church.[43]

In his own fashion—one not always appreciated by his pastors immersed in their confined local concerns—the bishop could justifiably make the same claim. Eight years later his episcopal record clearly confirmed his right to make it.

On the evening he and the head of state spoke from the same pulpit, they jointly announced to the world that "Mississippi's day of defiance was over." The years of "bitter-end resistance" to law and the moral imperatives of Wesleyan doctrine were nearing an end. The doors of "The Closed Society" and Methodist churches were to be opened, and Methodist laypersons including Robert L. Ezelle, Nat Rogers, Mrs. Karl Stauss and Clarie Collins Harvey were in the vanguard of "a new saliency in the state."[44] Methodism, observed the governor, had, since the days of Tobias Gibson, been "inseparably intertwined with the history of this state."[45]

A candid South Carolinian like Gibson, Pendergrass was a dogged strategist who brooked no interference with his episcopal business. Like his patron saint, "Pope John," he was a hard-bitten pragmatist. He seemed to welcome the title of "King Edward" bestowed upon him by his critics. He was convinced that church doors would be opened by practical men, not idealists. He was not above using others, if necessary, to accomplish goals for "the greater good," leaving little doubt about his convictions.[46]

A clear indication of his strategy occurred in September 1965 when a young black woman named Alfreda Donnan, a recent beauty contest winner in Natchez, applied for admission to Millsaps.[47] He waited for President Benjamin B. Graves and the trustees, including Nat Rogers, to approve her application. Only then did he add his endorsement of the highly controverted action. He was now free to announce to the world that this was no token gesture, and he assumed a leading role in the admission of Linda Ratliff during the summer term. He ignored protests by public figures and the threats of patrons of the school, and praised the trustees for abiding by the law of the land and the precepts of their Christian faith.[48]

When conference again convened in Galloway during June 1966 the bishop confronted his people with an issue of much larger dimensions than the admission of a black freshman to the all-white college: the final disposition of the all-black Central

Jurisdiction. He reminded those with short memories that in 1964 they had memorialized the General Conference to retain that adjunct body since "any kind of merger or mixing of the races" without "the consent of the local groups concerned" would result in "discord, disruption, and perhaps the unity of The Church." If, then, as Clay Foster Lee had warned at the time, the Mississippi Conference continued to withhold the necessary consent, the ultimate consequence would be no less than "an unthinkable calamity for Methodism."[49]

The moment of truth had now arrived. Was the conference morally bound to give her consent, or would she persist in her resistance to the change at the risk of a second separation from Mother Church? Faced with this dilemma, the conference finally submitted to Clay's appeal for a "Free Expression of All Options." After preachers and laypersons had bared their souls in public, the bishop's position was confirmed by a vote of 206 to 181 to abolish the Central Jurisdiction. Congratulatory telegrams poured in from New York, North Iowa, Central Illinois and elsewhere.[50] During the offertory an organ student from all-black Paine College in Augusta, Georgia, named for Mississippi-born Robert Paine, played "Fairest Lord Jesus."[51] His name was Norris Mackey.

In that same year Pendergrass and his staff inaugurated a sophisticated television program entitled "Venture in Action." No tax funds were involved, but the reputable firm of Marks and Lundy was retained to raise three million dollars from freewill offerings of the people. The North Mississippi Conference endorsed the project by a standing vote, and leaders of the two black conferences committed themselves to support the venture designed "to work for a Christian climate in our Area and to end 'Negativism' and begin the quest for 'Renewal.'"[52] Doubters may have wondered if Pendergrass had not been overawed by Norman Vincent Peale's *Power of Positive Thinking*.

The lasting fruits of "Venture" were as positive as they were notable. On the evening of June 13, 1968, a "Giant Victory Rally" was celebrated in Jackson's Municipal Auditorium. A choir of one hundred voices was recruited to accompany Bill Mann during his rendition of "He's Got the Whole World in His Hands." Representatives of the Roman Catholic and Protestant churches and Beth Israel Synagogue joined in the festivities. The "gallery" was not reserved for blacks. Black hands and white hands brought pledges totaling $3,493,458.65 and laid them on the improvised altar.[53]

Members of the Mississippi Association of Methodist Ministers and Laymen who came to "see the show" were stunned by the ecumenical "spectacle." They were witnessing a public repudiation of their gospel that racial integration was a "crime against God."[54] For their benefit the bishop announced that the General Conference had just mandated that United Methodism would be totally integrated by 1972, and that he had affixed his signature to the *edictum*.[55]

Probably no one present for that evening's celebration of joy suspected that within a brief period of time the campus of nearby Jackson State University would be converted into a battleground, May 13, 1970.[56] Nine days previously, four Kent State students were felled by fire from the carbines of National Guardsmen. Mississippians held their breath, awaiting further eruptions on the campuses at Lorman, Itta Bena, Oxford, Starkville and Hattiesburg, perhaps even Millsaps and Mississippi College. But it never happened. Campus pastors of all faiths, supported by churches northern critics labeled "racist," had undoubtedly assumed leading roles in holding back the gathering storm.[57]

Pendergrass' call for "Renewal" and the end of "Negativism" was part and parcel of the "New Directions" into which the state was turning during the administrations of John Bell Williams, William

Waller and Cliff Finch through the seventies.[58] Indeed, "religious organizations and the beliefs they propounded have always been a major cultural force in Mississippi." Yet it appears that little notice has been given to the new generation of Mississippi's Wesleyan moralists who forged the essential theological principles undergirding such beliefs propounded and their societal impact upon the emerging culture of the commonwealth.[59] Much more attention is given to the cultural influence of popular and sensitive novelists and essayists without whom, of course, Mississippi would be infinitely poorer.

Surely, Bishop Pendergrass, who is little known beyond the borders of the state and the confines of his church, should be assessed as a forger of moral forces lending character to the "New Directions." During his eight years as chief pastor his strategic utilization of his church's formidable human and institutional resources in building bulwarks against the ravaging tides of ignorance, racial discrimination, social upheaval and crimes against humanity committed in the name of law, profoundly impacted every segment of life in Mississippi. The founders of the Mississippi Religious Leadership Conference, one of whom was Catholic Bishop Joseph B. Brunini,[60] identified Pendergrass' "Catholic Spirit" with that of the legendary Galloway.[61]

John Wesley, the Anglo-Catholic, designed his itinerant "system" to adapt to the ever-changing climate of human society. Bishops (general superintendents) were little more than glorified circuit riders. They were never "settled" in one place indefinitely like Congregationalists.[62] When Pendergrass finished his assignment to Mississippi in 1972 he was succeeded by Mack B. Stokes.[63] Franklin had been a pastor to his people in trying times, and Pendergrass was a hard-hitting man of action. Stokes was a different breed.

He was the son of missionary parents in Korea,

and for the past three decades as professor of theology at Emory he had sent a procession of young theologs back to Mississippi. An academician, he was assigned to the conference as a "teaching bishop" whose unique gifts were deemed essential to cultivate the mental potentials of a highly activistic constituency. "Venture in Action" had been a necessary and commendable undertaking, but, without the stabilizing influence of education, action for action's sake might readily prove counterproductive. Citing the Oxford don, Stokes predicated his episcopacy on the principle that *eruditio et religio*, "knowledge and vital piety," were inseparable.[64]

Soon after assuming his new duties he quietly persuaded the conference leadership that Millsaps, the bastion of Methodist education in the state, should advance further along the path pioneered by Galloway and Murrah so that others besides undergraduates might "drink of our spring."[65] Largely due to his Attic persistence, and upon his recommendation, Clarie Collins Harvey was elected as the first black person to the board of trustees in 1974.[66]

At that time the two white conferences and the two black conferences in Mississippi were engaged in the unification process mandated by the General Conference of 1968. In view of the radical adjustments—a revolutionary psychological and demographic break from the past—the bishop and his council of advice thought it wise to dramatize the pending event for "people outside Mississippi" to view on television and follow in their newspapers. Their purpose, of course, was ideologically motivated; their strategy was an exercise in worldly-wise public relations. "People outside Mississippi" deserved a chance to change their distorted image of the racial climate in this land of incorrigible "rednecks."[67]

By 1978 conditions in the state appeared propitious for the move. For eight years court-ordered integration of the public schools had proceeded with such unexpected orderliness, especially in city systems such as Jackson, that one black principal, Lonnie King of Brinkley Junior High, exclaimed: "It seemed scientifically impossible."[68] During John Bell William's term as governor, 1968-1972, Robert L. Clark of Ebenezer was elected as the state's first black legislator since the end of Reconstruction. In the gubernatorial campaign of 1971 William Waller was challenged by Charles Evers of Fayette, the first black man to run for that office in the history of the state.[69]

It appeared that "Negativism" in Mississippi was breathing its last gasp—that "Renewal" was in the air. Having planned long and carefully for this visible change of the tide, the bishop and his colleagues rolled out the welcome mat of the Holiday Inn, downtown Jackson, to greet representatives of Black Methodists for Church Renewal during March 1978. The organization, numbering some 350,000 members in thirty-five states, was an official arm of The United Methodist Church created to serve as "the model of inclusiveness" for "an integrated church at all levels."[70] In addition to its purpose "to expose latent and overt forms of racism" in every segment of Methodist life, it was empowered by the General Conference "to encourage and involve Black Methodists and others in the struggle for economic and social justice."[71]

As the 1980s dawned, Bishop Stokes prepared to vacate the episcopal residence for his successor, Carlton P. Minnick.[72] The former Virginia businessman, educated for ministry in a Presbyterian seminary, inherited a people who through eighteen decades of struggle had often faltered in their mission to spread "scriptural holiness" across the land. They called themselves "extraordinary messengers" of the Lord. They excelled in evangelical strategy.[73]

They preached a rational faith that was scripturally centered but not biblically bound. They focused upon an imminent horizon that was "worldly" without being mundane. They were ideologues who refused to succumb to zeal that might consume their household.[74] They preached in the halls of government with the same freedom they enjoyed beneath the brush arbor. They mastered the art of politicizing principalities and those who sat in the seats of the mighty.[75]

Shoutin' Methodists never ceased to foster a firm familial tie with "the powers that be." Their frontier hero, Francis Asbury, wielded material moral force among the men who shaped the character of the American Commonwealth.[76] It was not by accident or a simple matter of convenient accessibility that the Constitutional Convention of 1817 convened in the old Methodist Church at Washington, Mississippi. Not a few of the delegates were either practicing Methodists or men who came under the influence of the circuit riders.[77]

In January 1980 that historical and emotional tie was symbolically reenacted in the capital city of the state. During an ecumenical, integrated service in Galloway Memorial, Governor William Winter, a Presbyterian elder, offered inaugural prayers under the watchful eye of the "proud bird of Jove."[78] Other grand sanctuaries were equally accessible.[79] Perhaps the selection was a subconscious recognition that, across the decades of deep dilemma and high euphoria in which the soul of the commonwealth had grown in grace, the role of Wesleyan stalwarts had been uncommonly crucial in shaping the Mississippi Character.

Perhaps it was a veiled confession by sensitive authorities that in moments when the destiny of this sovereign state and of the Republic had hung in the balance, Wesleyan men and women of stature refused to bend the knee to demagoguery. They had survived "in a hazardous, violent world by protest, ingenuity, and adaptability."[80]

Perhaps the distinguished statesmen and clerics of

many faiths who gathered in the sanctuary of Galloway were witnessing to the integrity of the "Gibson doctrine" of "a right judgment in all things." The man who came alone in a canoe to Natchez at the turn of the nineteenth-century was not concerned with the human origins of his converts, but rather with dreadful moral pitfalls awaiting them along their pilgrimage: sloth, greed, intellectual diffidence, political sham, the threat to any man's natural rights. Shoutin' Methodists down Mississippi way never took refuge in a "dream world" simply because they were busily engaged in "Praising the Lord!" They were a moral breed, born of conviction, bent to tasks "yet unresolved in American life."[81]

Epilog

America, the finer instincts of it, are in the very soul of Mississippi, and always have been.

Willie Morris

1 January 1799

Bishop Francis Asbury mustered his "spiritual cavalrymen" in Charleston, South Carolina, and commissioned a former slaveholder for mission to "The Natchez."

5 April 1804

Tobias Gibson was buried "in a family grave yard on a hill" some four miles south of Walnut Hills, later Vicksburg.

28 June 1935

The "lonely, unmarked grave" of a "weeping prophet" from Charleston was opened to the dawn's early light of a "New South," yielding only "a handful of dust and one fragment of bone" which was placed in a copper box on the grounds of Crawford Street Church, Vicksburg.

15 June 1980

On this balmy evening an integrated rally by Methodist preachers and people was conducted in the Coliseum, Jackson. Banners bearing the proclamation "A New Decade—A New Commitment" preceded a great cross being borne across the auditorium floor by a man and his wife, followed by the madding crowd along the "Way of Sorrows" while a quartet rendered a medley of sacred songs including "And Can It Be?"

"Could it be," asked the preacher of the evening, that "the blessings of yesterday will not suffice for today?" He had "a dream," he exclaimed, of "a million lay persons involved in evangelism in the next decade!" A scattering of muffled Amens was audible in the stands, but not a single shout was heard by expectant news reporters. The Methodists, quipped one disappointed newshawk, had not yet "gone to the mountain!"

16 June 1980

The bishop convened the Mississippi Annual Conference in the sanctuary where the governor had bowed his head in prayer six months earlier. Speaking directly to the liberally educated preachers who had sat at his feet, an Emory theologian raised his forefinger toward "Jove," soon to be regilded and positioned to breast every ill wind that blows. He then laid his hand on the open Bible and blessed this "house of prayer for all people" above whose stately columns

> the tempest's breath,
> the whirlwind's shock,
> have left untouched her hoary rock.

28 March 1983

State flags flew at half-mast in dignified tribute to a deceased governor often portrayed as a "racist." Fifty miles due north of the Capitol a "Coalition of Black Leaders of Holmes County" denounced church officials in New York for "shattering, instead of fostering, racial harmony" in Mississippi, including those involved in Global Ministries of the United Methodist Church.

Few Mississippians will likely remember this day or seriously reflect on the meaning of the parable. But it was a day on which the "finer instincts" buried in the soul of this commonwealth surfaced, if only momentarily, for a gainsaying world to ponder sober-mindedly. "A proud Mississippi has redeemed itself to a great extent and is now prepared to offer an example in human relations to the rest of the nation," declared Turner Catledge.

It is regrettable that the former editor of the *New York Times* and his Manhattan neighbor in the offices of Global Ministries could not have met to share their thoughts and reason together. But perhaps a higher authority has decreed that such a dialogue must first take place in Mississippi near the silt-covered footprint of Tobias Gibson forever buried in the mud of Natchez Landing.

Endnotes

Abbreviations

BHMM *Biographical and Historical Memoirs of Mississippi. . . . 2 vols. Chicago, 1891.*

CA *Christian Advocate (Southern CA, Western CA, etc.).*

CAJ *Christian Advocate and Journal.* New York, 1826 ff. Title varies.

HAM *The History of American Methodism.* Emory Stevens Bucke, ed. 3 vols. New York, Nashville, 1964.

HM *A History of Mississippi.* Richard Aubrey McLemore, ed. 2 vols. Hattiesburg, 1973.

JGC *Journal of the General Conference, 1796-1978:* The Methodist Episcopal Church, 1796-1938; the Methodist Episcopal Church, South, 1846-1938; the Methodist Protestant Church, 1832-1938.

JMC *Journal of the Mississippi Conference, 1813-1983.*

JMH *Journal of Mississippi History.* Jackson, 1939-1983.

JNMC *Journal of the North Mississippi Conference, 1871-1980.*

MMA *Mississippi Methodist Advocate.* Jackson, 1947-1983.

MQR *The Methodist Quarterly Review.* New York, Nashville, 1818-1939. Title varies.

NOCA *New Orleans Christian Advocate.* New Orleans, 1850-1980.

PMHS *Publications of the Mississippi Historical Society.* Jackson, 1898-1922.

Endnotes

One: Beachhead at Natchez Under-the-Hill

1. The precise date of Gibson's arrival is questionable. The Mississippi Territory was created by an Act of Congress, April 7, 1798. See Robert V. Haynes, in *HM* 1: 174-216. Also, Virginia P. Matthias, "Natchez Under-the-Hill as It Developed Under the Influence of the Mississippi River and the Natchez Trace," *JMH* 8 (Oct., 1954), 201-21.

2. Marcus Loane, *Oxford and the Evangelical Succession* (London, 1950); Maximin Piette, *John Wesley in the Evolution of Protestantism*. J. B. Howard, tr. (New York, 1937); Albert C. Outler, ed., *John Wesley* (New York, 1964).

3. John G. Jones, *A Complete History of Methodism as Connected with the Mississippi Conference of the Methodist Episcopal Church, South* (2 vols., Nashville, 1887) 1: 27; Benjamin M. Drake, "Tobias Gibson. The First Methodist Missionary to the Natchez Country," *MQR*, New Series 2 (May, 1887), 238-47; Gene Ramsey Miller, *A History of North Mississippi Methodism, 1820-1900* (Nashville, 1966).

4. Dawson A. Phelps, "Stands and Travel Accommodations on the Natchez Trace," *JMH* 11 (Jan., 1949), 1-54; D. Clayton James, *Antebellum Natchez* (Baton Rouge, 1968), 188.

5. William Winans, Autobiography, 62: Winans Papers, Millsaps-Wilson Library, Jackson; Jones, *Methodism* 1: 29; John F. H. Claiborne, *Mississippi as a Province, Territory, and State with Biographical Notices of Eminent Citizens* (Jackson, 1880), 209-10.

6. Z. T. Leavell, "Early Beginnings of Baptists in Mississippi," *PMHS* 4 (1901), 245-53; Richard A. McLemore, *A History of Mississippi Baptists, 1780-1970* (Jackson, 1971).

7. John Wesley, *A Treatise on Baptism* (London, 1756); Daniel Baker, *A Plain and Scriptural View of Baptism* (Philadelphia, 1853); Frederick R. Maser and George A. Singleton, in *HAM* 1: 631.

8. Jones, *Methodism* 1: 35.

9. *The Book of Common Prayer* (1928), 280; *The Methodist Discipline* (1858), 170.

10. Charles S. Sydnor, *Slavery in Mississippi* (New York, 1933); Eugene D. Genovese, *The World the Slaveholders Made: Two Essays in Interpretation* (New York, 1969); James Oakes, *The Ruling Race. A History of American Slaveholders* (New York, 1982).

11. Margaret D. Moore, ed., "Early Schools and Churches in Natchez," *JMH* 24 (Oct., 1962), 254-55; Jones, *Methodism* 1: 35-36.

12. Catharine C. Cleveland, *The Great Revival in the West, 1797-1804* (Gloucester, Mass., 1959).

13. Walter B. Posey, *The Development of Methodism in the Old Southwest, 1783-1824* (Tuscaloosa, 1933), 38-39; Peter Cartwright, *The Autobiography of Peter Cartwright* (Nashville, 1956), 91-92.

14. Jones, *Methodism* 1: 36.

15. Sydnor, *Slavery*, 223; Winans to Richmond Bledsoe, Aug. 22, 1834; Philip J. Staudenraus, *The African Colonization Movement, 1816-1865* (New York, 1961); Franklin L. Riley, "A Contribution to the History of the Colonization Movement in Mississippi," *PMHS* 9 (1906), 331-414.

16. "Liberty is the right of every human being, as soon as he breathes the vital air." John Wesley, *Thoughts upon Slavery* (London, 1774), 51.

17. Frank Baker, *Methodism and the Love-Feast* (London, 1957).

18. William Warren Sweet, ed., *The Rise of Methodism in the West: Being the Journal of the Western Conference, 1800-1811* (New York, 1920), proceedings for 1802, 1803; William Larkin Duren, *Francis Asbury* (New York, 1928).

19. "Elysian Fields" was located along the Amite-Wilkinson County line above the 31 degree parallel.

Floyd married Hannah Griffing of "sickly" St. Albans settlement. Winans, Diary, 1815; Jones, *Methodism* 1: 55.

20. Jones, *Methodism* 1: 47-48.

21. *Minutes of the Annual Conferences of the Methodist Episcopal Church, 1773-1845* (3 vols., New York, 1840-1846) 1: 125-26.

22. Winans to Benjamin M. Drake, May 12, 1857; Jones, *Methodism* 1: 108-13; Henry Gabriel Hawkins, *Methodism in Natchez. Including "A Centennial Retrospect or Methodism in Natchez, Miss., from 1799 to 1884, by W. C. Black"* (Jackson, 1937), 20-22.

23. Elijah Embree Hoss, *William McKendree. A Biographical Study* (Nashville, 1916), 82-87; Robert Paine, *Life and Times of William M'Kendree* (2 vols., Nashville, 1869); McKendree Papers, Vanderbilt University, Emory University.

24. Jones, *Methodism* 1: 114-17.

25. Lerner (Learner) Blackman, Journal, 32 pp. Winans Papers, Millsaps-Wilson Library, Jackson. See Abel Stevens, *History of the Methodist Episcopal Church in the United States of America* (4 vols., New York, 1867) 4: 379.

26. E. Brooks Holifield, *The Gentlemen Theologians. American Theology in Southern Culture, 1795-1860* (Durham, 1978), 16-17; William Warren Sweet, *Methodism in American History* (New York, 1933), 104-05.

27. Hawkins, *Methodism in Natchez*, 28.

28. Lorenzo Dow, *History of Cosmopolite; or the Four Volumes of Lorenzo's Journal* (New York, 1814); Charles B. Galloway, "Lorenzo Dow in Mississippi," *PMHS* 4 (1901), 233-44.

29. Blackman, Journal, Oct.-Nov., 1804; Winans, Autobiography, 65; Robert S. Cotterill, "The Natchez Trace," *Louisiana Historical Quarterly* 6 (April, 1923), 259-68.

30. The origin of this local church council is unknown. See Jesse Lee, *A Short History of the Methodists in the United States of America* (Baltimore, 1810), 41-42.

31. Jones, *Methodism* 1: 122-23; Stevens *History* 4: 114, 158, 349, 356, 432; Charles A. Johnson, *The Frontier Camp Meeting, Religion's Harvest Time* (Dallas, 1955); Camp meetings were like "fishing with a large net." Asbury to Thornton Fleming, Dec. 2, 1802. See note 75 below. Also, Holifield, *Gentlemen Theologians*, 142, on "conviction."

32. One of these vigorous exercises was "the jerks." John W. Monette, *History of the Discovery and Settlement of the Valley of the Mississippi* (2 vols., New York, 1848) 2: 29; Winans, Autobiography, 13.

33. During one camp meeting a Baptist arrived with a wagonload of whiskey barrels, quickly sold out, and "many got groggy." John Lyle, Diary, 1801-1803. Durrett Collection, University of Chicago.

34. Claiborne, *Mississippi*, 194n, 376; Madel J. Morgan, "Andrew Marschalk's Account of Mississippi's First Press," *JMH* 8 (July, 146-48.

35. Cleveland, *The Great Revival*, 53, 120; Richard McNemar, *The Kentucky Revival* (Cincinnati, 1807).

36. Jones, *Methodism* 1: 124.

37. Dow, *History of Cosmopolite*, 212; Hawkins, *Methodism in Natchez*, 25.

38. William B. Hamilton, "Jefferson College and Education in Mississippi, 1798-1817," *JMH* 3 (Oct., 1949), 259-76.

39. Jones, *Methodism* 1: 126-28.

40. Whatcoat, Journal. Garrett Theological Seminary Library, Evanston. See Benjamin St. James Fry, *Richard Whatcoat* (New York, 1852).

41. Jack D. L. Holmes, in *HM* 1: 169; Robert V. Haynes, *ibid.* 1: 244n.

42. Cloud "located in 1811. Nothing further is known of him." Hawkins, *Methodism in Natchez*, 29.

43. Posey, *Old Southwest*, 44; Jones, *Methodism* 1: 154-56.

44. Philander Chase, *Reminiscences: An Autobiography* . . . (2 vols., Boston, 1848).

45. Elisha Bowman to William Burke, Jan. 29, 1806, quoted in *NOCA*, April 12, 1851, p. 2.

46. Jones, *Methodism* 1: 148-52.

47. John M. Barker, *History of Ohio Methodism* (Cincinnati, 1898).

48. McKendree was known as the "Lion of the West." Sweet, *Methodism in American History*, 166; Hoss, *McKendree*, 106-10.

49. Bowman to William Burke, Jan. 29, 1806.

50. Gibson was buried "in a plain, primitive Christian style." Vicksburg *Evening Post*, July 2, 1935.

51. Hawkins, *Methodism in Natchez*, 29.

52. Blackman, Journal, chap. 8; Jones, *Methodism* 1: 171-83.

53. Jacob Young, *Autobiography of a Pioneer* . . . (Cincinnati, 1857); *Western CA*, Sept. 12, 1845.

54. Jones, *Methodism* 1: 201.

55. John N. Norwood, *The Schism in the Methodist Episcopal Church, 1844: A Study of Slavery and Ecclesiastical Politics* (Alfred, 1923); Donald G. Mathews, *Slavery and Methodism: A Chapter in American Morality, 1780-1845* (Princeton, 1965); Abel Stevens, *The Life and Times of Nathan Bangs* (New York, 1863).

56. Hoss, *McKendree*, 107; Holifield, *Gentlemen Theologians*, 119.

57. Winans, Autobiography, 56-57; Jones, *Methodism* 1: 207.

58. *Journal of the Western Conference*, proceedings for 1810.

59. Stevens, *History* 4: 154; Lawrence Sherwood, in *HAM* 1: 404.

60. Winans, Autobiography, 63; Margaret D. Moore, "Protestantism in the Mississippi Territory," *JMH* 29 (Nov., 1967), 358-70.

61. Jones, *Methodism* 1: 207-12.

62. Anson West, *A History of Methodism in Alabama* (Nashville, 1892); Jones, *Methodism* 1: 125-26, 219-27.

63. The Natchez region had begun to assume the look of "a permanent ministerial home" and "self-supporting establishment." Jones, *Methodism* 1: 215-16.

64. *Journal of the Western Conference*, proceedings

for 1810.

65. Winans, Autobiography, 62.

66. James, *Antebellum Natchez*, 156, 240.

67. Winans, Autobiography, 123-24; Joseph D. Shields, *Natchez: Its Early History*. Elizabeth D. Murray, ed. (Louisville, 1930), 84.

68. During fever epidemics "perhaps more than half of every family" was "prostrate with sickness," the atmosphere "reeking with pestilence." Winans, Autobiography, 72-75.

69. Claiborne, *Mississippi*, 347-48n.

70. Winans, Autobiography, 81-82.

71. "How deep must be the depravity of the heart which could conceive such a scheme! And, how great the public credulity that could render such a scheme successful!" Winans, Autobiography, 83.

72. Eron Rowland, *Andrew Jackson's Campaign Against the British, or the Mississippi Territory in the War of 1812* . . . (New York, 1926). The Union "was saved by the weakness of its enemies far more than by its own strength." Alexis de Tocqueville, *Democracy in America* (2 vols., New York, 1908) 1: 172n.

73. Jones, *Methodism* 1: 234-35.

74. *JGC*, 1812, pp. 108-109; Miller, *North Mississippi Methodism*, 13-15.

75. *The Journal and Letters of Francis Asbury*. Elmer T. Clark, J. Manning Potts and Jacob S. Payton, ed. (3 vols., Nashville, 1958): Journal entry, Nov. 1-12, 1812.

76. Albert J. Pickett, *History of Alabama and Incidentally of Georgia and Mississippi from the Earliest Period* (2 vols. in one, revised, Charleston, 1962), 528-43.

77. Robert V. Haynes, in *HM* 1: 228-31.

78. Winans, Autobiography, 85.

79. Jones, *Methodism* 1: 302-44.

80. Winans, Autobiography, 85-89; Jones, *Methodism*, 1: 305-18. The manuscript journal measures 7 ½ by 6 inches (1813-1837, one year missing). Methodist Archives, Millsaps-Wilson-Library, Jackson.

81. Winans, Autobiography, 97-103; H. C. Jen-

nings, *The Methodist Book Concern: A Romance of History* (New York, Cincinnati, 1924); Ray Holder, "Methodist Beginnings in New Orleans, 1813-1814," *Louisiana History* 18 (Spring, 1977), 171-82; Timothy F. Reilly, "Slavery and the Southwestern Evangelist in New Orleans (1800-1861)," *JMH* 41 (Nov., 1979), 301-17.

82. Jones, *Methodism* 1: 325-26, 344, 365-85; Eron Rowland, "The Mississippi Territory in the War of 1812," *PMHS*, Centenary Series 4 (1921), 7-233.

83. Winans, Autobiography, 116-17.

84. Matthew H. Moore, *Sketches of the Pioneers of Methodism in North Carolina and Virginia* (Nashville, 1884), 280-90; Winans, Autobiography, 114-15; Jones, *Methodism* 1: 373-79.

85. Winans, Diary, March 21, 1815.

86. Robert V. Remini, *Andrew Jackson and the Course of American Empire, 1767-1821* (New York, 1977).

87. Winans, Autobiography, 117-19; Jones, *Methodism* 1: 382.

88. Robert V. Haynes, quoting George Poindexter, in *HM* 1: 227.

89. Arrell M. Gibson, in *HM* 1: 85.

90. Winans, Autobiography, 89-91.

91. *Ibid.*, 117.

Two: Breakout to the Bayous and Piney Woods

1. Francis A. and James A. Cabaniss, "Religion in Antebellum Mississippi," *JMH* 6 (Oct., 1944), 191-224.

2. James J. Pillar, in *HM* 1: 378-92.

3. A few of these "modest and self-distrusting young ministers doubted their authority to hold a legal Conference." Jones, *Methodism* 1: 310.

4. *Minutes of Several Conversations Between the Rev. Thomas Coke, LL.D., the Rev. Francis Asbury, and Others,*

at a Conference, Begun in Baltimore, in the State of Maryland, on Monday, the 27th of December, in the Year 1784 . . .(Philadelphia, 1785); Norman W. Spellman, in *HAM* 1: 185-232.

5. John W. Parris, *John Wesley's Doctrine of the Sacraments* (London, 1963); Victor E. Vine, "'Episcope' in Methodism," *Proceedings of the Wesley Historical Society* 30 (1956), 162-170.

6. Jones, *Methodism* 1: 390.

7. The journal, not the conference, was lost. Jones, *Methodism* 1: 387.

8. Donald M. Rawson, "Democratic Resurgence in Mississippi, 1852-1853," *JMH* 25 (Feb., 1964), 1-27; Jones, *Methodism* 1: 391.

9. Winans, Diary, March 8—Sept. 14, 1815.

10. Jones, *Methodism* 1: 411.

11. Having lost the "desire to flee from the wrath to come" following the war, some 175 whites and 100 blacks abandoned the church. Jones, *Methodism* 1: 416.

12. Never considered "a preacher of high order," Asbury was "probably never excelled" in the art of "ecclesiastical government." Winans, Autobiography, 57-58.

13. Charles Elliott, *The Life of Rev. Robert R. Roberts* (New York, 1844); Benjamin St. James Fry, *Enoch George* (New York, 1852); Roberts, Autobiography. DePauw University.

14. Winans, Autobiography, 127.

15. Jones, *Methodism* 1: 425-27.

16. *JMC*, 1980, p. 149, noting a 500% increase in giving.

17. T. L. Haman, "Beginnings of Presbyterianism in Mississippi," *PMHS* 10 (1909), 204-16.

18. Winans, Autobiography, 129; Claiborne, *Mississippi*, 352-60; W. Magruder Drake, "Mississippi's First Constitutional Convention," *JMH* 18 (April, 1956), 79-110.

19. W. Magruder Drake, "The Framing of Mississippi's First Constitution," JMH 29 (Nov., 1965), 301-

27; J. B. Cain, *Methodism in the Mississippi Conference, 1846-1870* (Jackson, 1939), 157.

20. Winans, *Autobiography*, 130-31.

21. In 1820 conference membership numbered 3,433 whites and 686 blacks; one year later the figures rose to 4,531 and 1,020 respectively. *JMC*, 1820-1821, statistical tables.

22. Winans, *Autobiography*, 131-35; Jones, *Methodism* 2: 22-23.

23. Winans, *Autobiography*, 132-33.

24. Eli Truitt to William McKendree, Aug. 27, 1822. McKendree Papers, Vanderbilt University Library.

25. Winans, *Autobiography*, 141-43.

26. Charles B. Galloway, "Elizabeth Female Academy—the Mother of Female Colleges," *PMHS* 2 (1899), 169-78; Catherine Clinton, *The Plantation Mistress* . . . (New York, 1982,) 129-30.

27. Winans, *Autobiography*, 144.

28. *Ibid.*, 163-64.

29. *Ibid.*, 168-69; Jones, *Methodism* 2: 25-27. Governor McRae's steamboat was named *Triumph*. David G. Sansing and Carroll Waller, *A History of the Mississippi Governor's Mansion* (Jackson, 1977), 40.

30. Winans, *Autobiography*. 161.

31. "Probably the most effective evangelical program among Negroes in Mississippi was that of the Natchez Methodist Church." James, *Antebellum Natchez*, 247. See Dickson D. Bruce, Jr., *And They All Sang Hallelujah: Plain-Folk Camp-Meeting Religion* (Knoxville, 1974).

32. Wade Crawford Barclay, *The History of Methodist Missions* (3 vols., New York, 1949-1957).

33. Winans, *Autobiography*, 175, apparently alluding to Asbury's exclamation: "Ride on, blessed Redeemer, until all states and nations are subdued unto thy sacred way"! Asbury, *Journal*, May 23, 1802.

34. Winans, *Autobiography*, 177-78.

35. *Ibid.*, 188; Jones, *Methodism* 2: 31-36. See studies on yellow fever, in Franklin L. Riley, "Life and Lit-

erary Services of Dr. John W. Monette," *PMHS* 9 (1909), 199-237. Monette and his physician-father, Samuel Wesley, were local preachers.

36. McKendree strongly emphasized mission to Indians and slaves. Paine, *McKendree* 1: 403.

37. Jones, *Methodism* 2: 31-36.

38. Winans, Autobiography, 184-88.

39. *Ibid.*, 188-208.

40. Edward J. Drinkhouse, *History of Methodist Reform . . . with Reference to . . . the Methodist Protestant Church* (2 vols., Baltimore, Pittsburgh, 1899).

41. Davis W. Clark, *Life and Times of Elijah Hedding . . .* (New York, 1855); Horace M. Du Bose, *The Life of Joshua Soule* (Nashville, 1911).

42. Winans, Journal, May 26-27, 1824.

43. *Ibid.*, May 11, 26, 1824. After 1822 a special act of the Mississippi Legislature was required before a slave could be manumitted for African colonization or removed to a free state. Anderson Hutchinson, comp., *Revised Code of the Statutes of Mississippi* (Jackson, 1848, 1857), 523.

44. Winans to Ashley Hewit (Hewitt), Aug. 4, 1824; Florence Rebecca Ray, *Chieftain Greenwood LeFlore and the Choctaw Indians of the Mississippi Valley* (Memphis, 1936); Andrew Badger, "A Brief History of the Choctaw Language," *JMH* 40 (Feb., 1978), 49-59.

45. Winans, Journal, Dec. 23-30, 1824; April 2, 9-11, 1825.

46. Winans to Joshua Soule, April 22, 1825; Percy L. Rainwater, "Indian Missions and Missionaries," *JMH* 28 (Feb., 1966), 15-39.

47. Jones, *Methodism* 2: 165.

48. Ronald N. Satz, *American Indian Policy in the Jacksonian Era* (Lincoln, 1975); Francis F. Prucha, "Andrew Jackson's Indian Policy: A Reassessment," *Journal of American History* 56 (1969), 527-39.

49. Robert V. Remini, *Andrew Jackson and the Course of American Freedom, 1822-1832* (New York, 1981), 257-79.

50. Jones, *Methodism* 2: 165-86.

51. *Ibid.* 2: 178-81.

52. *Ibid.* 2: 200; Soule, in *MQR* 11 (1828), 79.

53. Winans to William Lattimore, March 16, 1830.

54. Winans to Alexander Talley, Aug. 17, 1830. See excerpts from Brandon's inaugural, in Dunbar Rowland, *Mississippi: The Heart of the South* (4 vols., Chicago, Jackson, 1925) 1: 553.

55. *Hutchinson's Code* (1848), 135-36; Claiborne, *Mississippi*, 510; *Mississippi Session Acts* (Jackson, 1829), 81-83.

56. Jones, *Methodism* 2: 205, 227; Posey, *Old Southwest*, 81-90; Henry S. Halbert, "Story of the Treaty of Dancing Rabbit," *PMHS* 6 (1902), 375-402; Arthur H. DeRosier, Jr., *The Removal of the Choctaw Indians* (Knoxville, 1970); a memoir of Smith, in *JMC*, 1845, p. 33.

57. William H. Milburn, *The Pioneers, Preachers, and People of the Mississippi Valley* (New York, 1860), 457-58.

58. Jones, *Methodism* 2: 185-86, 241-42.

59. Winans, Journal, Oct. 9, 1826; Winans to Benjamin M. Drake, Nov. 7, 1826.

60. Winans, Journal, Dec. 17, 1826; Jones, *Methodism* 2: 87-89, 114-32.

61. Winans, Journal, May 12-24, 1828; Douglass R. Chandler, in *HAM* 1: 649-52; Hoss, *McKendree*, 175-96.

62. Winans, Journal, Oct. 10, 27, 1828.

63. Jones, *Methodism* 2: 186.

64. Walter B. Posey, *Religious Strife on the Southern Frontier* (Baton Rouge, 1965).

65. Winans, Journal, Oct. 29. 1828.

66. Jones, *Methodism* 2: 273-74.

67. *JMC*, 1829, statistical notation, churchwide.

68. Winans to John Gibson, Feb. 6, 1830.

69. Winans to William Lattimore, Feb. 16, 1830.

70. *Ibid.*; Winans to John R. Nicholson, Sept. 14, 1830. See James Oliver Robertson, *American Myth, American Reality* (New York, 1980), 75.

71. Winans to Nicholson, Sept. 14, 1830.

72. *Journal of the Convention of the State of Mississippi Held in the Town of Jackson* (Jackson, 1832); Edwin A. Miles, *Jacksonian Democracy in Mississippi* (Chapel Hill, 1960), 20-32.

73. Politicians were often first to pitch their tents on the campground. Ralph L. Rusk, *The Literature of the Middle Western Frontier* (2 vols., New York, 1925) 1: 47.

74. Winans to Nicholson, Sept. 14, 1830.

75. "The intention of the legislature *was* oppression," and those who thought otherwise "ought to be confined" under "a charge of mental imbecility." Winans to Lattimore, March 16, 1830.

76. Charles B. Galloway, "Thomas Griffin: A Boanerges of the Early Southwest," *PMHS* 7 (1903), 153-70.

77. Winans to Caroline M. Thayer, Oct. 7, 1830.

78. Angie Nebo, *The Rise and Fall of the Choctaw Republic* (Norman, 1934); James W. Silver, "A Counter-Proposal to the Indian Policy of Andrew Jackson," *JMH* 4 (Oct., 1942), 207-15.

79. Grant Foreman, *Indian Removal: The Emigration of the Five Civilized Tribes of Indians* (Norman, 1932).

80. *JMC*, 1830, pp. 1-2; Jones, *Methodism* 2: 262.

Three: Defenders Against the Yankee Threat

1. Claiborne, *Mississippi*, 515.

2. The "many striking instances" of the Indians' ability to engage in "the pursuits of civilized life" could not be ignored by white men. Winans to Alexander Talley, Aug. 17, 1830.

3. Politicians and land speculators rejoiced that red men would readily "sell all that was dearest to them for a few gallons" of whiskey. Winans to Talley, Aug. 17, 1830; Debo, *Rise and Fall of the Choctaw Republic*, 48.

4. Claiborne, *Mississippi*, 509.

5. Bishop Roberts permitted nothing, including the educational efforts of the preachers, "to be done with carelessness." Jones, *Methodism* 2: 274-77.

6. Winans to Talley, Jan. 14, 1832. See Norwood Allen Kerr, "The Mississippi Colonization Society (1831-1860)," *JMH* 43 (Feb., 1981), 1-30.

7. West, *Methodism in Alabama, passim;* Barclay, *Methodist Missions* 2: 112-69; Jones, *Methodism* 2: 280.

8. John B. McFerrin, *History of Methodism in Tennessee* (3 vols., Nashville, 1873).

9. "Little Tommy" Owens' "native wit" often threw the preachers "into convulsive laughter." Jones, *Methodism* 2: 420-21; Cain, *Methodism*, 445-46.

10. Foreman, *Indian Removal*, 193-200; Dawson A. Phelps, "The Chickasaw Mission," *JMH* 13 (Nov., 1951), 226-35; Arrell M. Gibson, *The Chickasaws* (Norman, 1971).

11. James, *Antebellum Natchez*, 113.

12. Winans to David Gordon, Dec. 7, 1831; to Spence M. Grayson, Sept. 17, 1832.

13. David H. Markle, "Wilbur Fisk, Pioneer Methodist Educator" (Ph. D. dissertation, Yale University, 1935); Joseph Holdich, *The Life of Wilbur Fisk, D. D.* (New York, 1842); Carl F. Price, *Wesleyan's First Century* (Middletown, 1932); Winans to Fisk, Aug. 2, 1833.

14. In the proper theological training of their men for mission, "no other denomination in America was more backward" than the Methodists. William R. Cannon, in *HAM* 1: 571.

15. Jones, *Methodism* 2: 274-77. See Richard Hofstadter, *Anti-Intellectualism in American Life* (New York, 1966), 55-141.

16. Robert Emory, *The Life of Rev. John Emory* (New York, 1841, 1844), 265-66.

17. Jones, *Methodism* 2: 314-15; W. H. Weathersby, "A History of Mississippi College," *PMHS*, Centenary Series 5 (1922), 184-99; Melerson G. Dunham, *Centennial History of Alcorn A. & M. College*

(Hattiesburg, 1971).

18. William H. Nelson, *A Burning Torch and A Flaming Fire: The Story of Centenary College* (Nashville, 1908), 97-135; Ray Holder, "Centenary: Roots of a Pioneer College (1838-1844)," *JMH* 43 (May, 1980), 77-98.

19. Population of the state increased from 70,443 in 1830 to 179,074 in 1840. *Census of Population*, 1840, p. 45.

20. Wendell P. and Francis J. Garrison, *William Lloyd Garrison, 1805-1879* (4 vols., Boston, 1885-1889).

21. Winans, Autobiography, 126-27; Theodore Bourne, "George Bourne, The Pioneer of American Antislavery," *MQR* 64 (Jan., 1882), 69-73.

22. Claiborne, *Mississippi*, 145.

23. Quoted in Sydnor, *Slavery*, 239.

24. Claiborne, *Mississippi*, 386.

25. Jones, *Methodism* 2: 346.

26. Benjamin M. Drake, John Lane and William Winans were delegates; William M. Curtiss and Benjamin A. Houghton, reserves. Jones, *Methodism* 2: 349.

27. *The Methodist Discipline* (Church, South, 1858), 102.

28. Winans to Joshua Soule, Nov. 28, 1834; Jones, *Methodism* 2: 339-49.

29. Thomas L. Williams, "The Methodist Mission to the Slaves" (Ph. D. dissertation, Yale University, 1943); William P. Harrison, ed., *The Gospel Among the Slaves* (Nashville, 1893).

30. Jones, *Methodism*, 2: 346-47. See Mathews, *Slavery and Methodism*; Dwight W. Culver, *Negro Segregation in the Methodist Church* (New Haven, 1953); Lucius C. Matlack, *The Antislavery Struggle and Triumph in the Methodist Episcopal Church* (New York, 1881); H. Shelton Smith, *In His Image, But . . . Racism in Southern Religion, 1780-1910* (Durham, 1972), 94-114.

31. Winans to Obadiah Winans, Dec. 23, 1836.

32. Edwin A. Miles, "The Mississippi Slave Insur-

rection Scare of 1834," *Journal of Negroe History* 42 (Jan., 1957), 48-60.

33. Winans to William Dowsing, June 7, 1836. The resolution, "carefully and elaborately" drafted by Winans, defined Mississippi's position on abolitionism and "the relation of ministers of the gospel to the civil institutions of the country." Jones, *Methodism* 2: 346-47.

34. Winans to Obadiah Winans, Dec. 26, 1836. See Lucius C. Matlack, *The Life of Orange Scott* . . . (New York, 1847-1848).

35. John F. Marley, *The Life of Rev. Thomas A. Morris* (Cincinnati, 1875).

36. Winans to Wilbur Fisk, June 30, 1837.

37. Sydnor, *Slavery*, 243.

38. Miller, *North Mississippi Methodism*, 43-44.

39. The Mississippi Conference "still kept watch over the rich harvest soon to be reaped by missionary operations in Texas" initiated by Robert Alexander, Littleton Fowler and Martin Ruter. Jones, *Methodism* 2: 368-70. See Earnest A. Smith, *Martin Ruter* (New York, Cincinnati, 1915).

40. Winans, Journal, May 1-31, 1840.

41. Thomas C. Thornton, *Inaugural Address Delivered at the First Commencement of Centenary College* (Jackson, 1842); Tommy W. Rogers, "T. C. Thornton: A Methodist Educator of Antebellum Mississippi," *JMH* 44 (May, 1982), 136-46.

42. Reginald C. McGrane, *The Panic of 1837* (Chicago, 1924); James, *Antebellum Natchez*, 202-03; Sydnor, *Slavery*, 165-66; Jones, *Methodism* 2: 372-75.

43. Donald G. Mathews, in Martin B. Duberman, ed., *The Antislavery Vanguard: New Essays on the Abolitionists* (Princeton, 1965), 70-101; Ralph Volney Harlow, *Gerrit Smith, Philanthropist and Reformer* (New York, 1939); Lucius C. Matlack, *History of The Wesleyan Methodist Connection of America* (New York, 1849).

44. Winans to Gerrit Smith, Nov. 18, 1837.

45. Winans to Frederick A. W. Davis, Nov. 8, 1841; Natchez *Mississippi Free Trader*, May 23, 1840.

46. Winans to Elijah Steele, May 9, 1840; to Obadiah Winans, June 8, 1840. See *Hutchinson's Code*, 533; *JGC*, 1840, pp. 71, 113-26, 142-43; *Western CA*, July 3, 1840, p. 41.

47. Winans to Enoch N. Talley, July 30, 1840; Jones, *Methodism* 2: 442-43; William Wightman, *The Life of William Capers, D. D.* (Nashville, 1858, 1902); *Proceedings of the Meeting in Charleston, S. C., May 13-15, 1845, on the Religious Instruction of the Negroes, etc.* (Charleston, 1845).

48. George G. Smith, *The Life and Letters of James Osgood Andrew* (Nashville, 1883).

49. Jones, *Methodism* 2: 440-41.

50. *JMC*, 1840, pp. 4-7; Jones, *Methodism* 2: 441.

51. A committee was appointed "to take into consideration the best method of giving religious instruction to the colored people," and to publish a catechism to be used by "the pastors of colored people" for the instruction of both black and white children. Contrary to state law, the pastors were directed to teach "additional lessons"—reading and writing—to black children. Jones, *Methodism* 2: 442-43; *BHMM* 2: 96; *Hutchinson's Code*, 948. See Charles C. Jones, *The Religious Instruction of Slaves in the United States* (Savannah, 1842).

52. Joseph Mitchell, "Traveling Preacher and Settled Farmer," *Methodist History* 5 (July, 1967), 7; *JGC*, 1844, pp. 63-66, 83-84, 186-205; *Report of Debates in the General Conference of the Methodist Episcopal Church, Held in the City of New York* (New York, 1844), 109-75.

53. Winans to Charles K. Marshall, Aug. 27, 1841.

54. Benjamin M. Drake, *A Sketch of the Life of Rev. Elijah Steele, and A Funeral Discourse by W. Winans, D. D.* (Cincinnati, 1843).

55. Charles S. Sydnor, *The Development of Southern Sectionalism, 1819-1848* (Baton Rouge, 1948, 1968), 338.

56. Daniel DeVinne to William Winans, Jan. 5, 1841; Winans to DeVinne, Aug. 31, 1841.

57. Jones, *Methodism* 2: 482-504.

58. Henry B. Ridgaway, *The Life of Edmund S. Janes* . . . (New York, Cincinnati, 1882).

59. Jones, *Methodism* 2: 485-86.

60. *JGC*, 1844, pp. 135-37; Winans to Obadiah Winans, June 28, 1844; to Maria O. Huston, June 5, 7, 1844.

61. Winans to Martha L. Gibson, June 28, 1844.

62. Winans to William H. Watkins, July 11, 1844; to Needham B. Raiford, July 22, 1844.

63. Winans to Raiford, July 22, 1844.

64. Winans, Journal, Dec. 11-20, 1844; Jones, *Methodism* 2: 503-26. See Joseph B. Stratton, *Memorial of a Quarter-Century's Pastorate* (Philadelphia, 1869), 55-56.

65. Winans to Maria O. Huston, March 13, 1845; Jones, *Methodism* 2: 510-15; *History of the Organization of the Methodist Episcopal Church, South* . . . (Nashville, 1845), 169-236.

66. Carl N. Degler, *The Other South. Southern Dissenters in the Nineteenth Century* (New York, 1974), 1-10.

67. Nolan B. Harmon, in *HAM* 2: 130-43; Cain, *Methodism*, 1-6.

68. Winans to Thomas A. Morris, June 28, 1845; to DeVinne, July 1, 1845.

69. Winans to Henry Clay, May 24, 1845.

70. Winans to Mary S. Wall, May 17, 18, 1846; to William H. Watkins, June 24, 1846; *CAJ*, May 20, 1862, p. 162.

71. Reuben Davis, *Recollections of Mississippi and Mississippians* (Revised edn., Hattiesburg, 1972), 270-73.

72. Winans to Mary S. Wall, May 18, 1846.

73. Robert Henry Harper, *Louisiana Methodism* (Washington, 1949).

74. Winans to Malachi DuBose, Sept. 11, 1846; to Mrs. Samuel Williams, Sept. 23, 1846; Cain, *Methodism*, 11.

75. Winans to John G. Richardson, Oct. 26, 1846.

76. Winans to Benjamin L. C. Wailes, Nov. 16, 1848; Cain, *Methodism*, 25, 29, 31-38.

77. Winans to Augustus B. Longstreet, March 27, 1850; James B. Murphy, *L. Q. C. Lamar: Pragmatic Patriot* (Baton Rouge, 1973); John Donald Wade, *Augustus Baldwin Longstreet: A Study of the Development of Culture in the South* (New York, 1924); Nash K. Burger and John K. Bettersworth, in Dean Faulkner Wells and Hunter Cole, ed., *Mississippi Heroes* (Jackson, 1980), 107-42.

78. David M. Key, "Historical Sketch of Millsaps College," Millsaps College *Bulletin*, 30 (Dec., 1946), 6-24.

79. Allen Cabaniss, *The University of Mississippi. Its First Hundred Years* (Second edn., Hattiesburg, 1971), 60-63, 80-81, 96, 99, 100.

80. Arthur E. Jones, Jr., in *HAM* 2: 144-205.

81. *CAJ*, Feb. 4, 1846, p. 102; R. Sutton, *The Methodist Property Case* (New York, 1851); Winans to Maria O. Huston, Jan. 18; Dec. 11, 1846; Oct. 28, 1847; March 27, 1849. "It would be proper for those who wish to adhere either North or South to do so without molestation or reproach: but, management and agitation, with a view to produce such adherence, or to prevent it . . . I consider pernicious." Winans to George C. M. Roberts, Feb. 8, 1850.

82. *JGC*, 1846, p. 101. See George G. Smith, *The Life and Times of George Foster Pierce . . . With His Sketch of His Father, Lovick Pierce, With an Introduction by A. G. Haygood* (Sparta, Ga., 1888).

83. *Daily CA*, May 6, 1848.

84. Quoted in Paul Neff Garber, *The Methodists Are One People* (Nashville, 1939), 58.

85. Winans to James C. Finley, June 21, 1848.

86. If Pierce failed "to get himself formally recognized," he would presumably make "his rejection a key issue in the conflict between the two churches." Arthur E. Jones, Jr., in *HAM* 2: 172-73.

87. Norwood, *Schism in the Methodist Church*, 124-25; Winans to Harper and Bros., July 20, 1848.

88. Any woman not willing to share the poverty of a circuit rider would be "a fool *par excellence*" to

marry him. Winans to Maria O. Huston, Dec. 11, 1846.

89. The Constitution of Cane Ridge Sunday School, 1850. Fayette Circuit Records, Methodist Archives, Millsaps-Wilson Library.

90. Cain, *Methodism*, 39, 45; Tommy W. Rogers, "The Schools of Higher Learning at Sharon, Mississippi," *JMH* 28 (Feb., 1966), 40-55.

91. Samuel L. L. Scott was the preacher. Henry J. Harris, Autobiography. Methodist Archives, Millsaps-Wilson Library.

Four: Survivors of the Eye of the Storm

1. Cain, *Methodism*, 50-59.

2. Allan Nevins, *Ordeal of the Union. Fruits of Manifest Destiny, 1847-1852* (2 vols., New York, 1947) 1: 219.

3. Hiram Mattison, *The Impending Crisis of 1860* (New York, 1859).

4. James B. Ranck, *Albert Gallatin Brown, Radical Southern Nationalist* (New York, 1937); Augustus B. Longstreet to William Winans, Feb. 28, 1850; Winans to Longstreet, March 27, 1850; to Benjamin M. Drake, Feb. 25, 1850.

5. Prior to 1850 "the South had furnished the most informed critics of the institution of slavery itself," but during the ensuing decade she "committed almost every political error in the book." T. Harry Williams, *Romance and Realism in Southern Politics* (Baton Rouge, 1966), 10.

6. "Old Bullet" Longstreet recommended that, unless "God interpose," the South should prepare to defend her rights, if necessary, with military force. *A Voice from the South: Comprising Letters from Georgia to Massachusetts, and to the Southern States* (Baltimore, 1847), 57-58.

7. "Our Country has been convulsed, right side up. No thanks, however, if this be so, to our [John

A.] Quitman" and other Mississippi Fire-Eaters. Winans to Jefferson Hamilton, Nov. 16, 1850. "What, then, can the Slave-holding States do? Let them . . . cling to the Union and the Constitution." A "dissolution of the Union" would "be Pandora's Box opened" with "a vengeance." Winans to Charles K. Marshall, Dec. 2, 1856. See John F. H. Claiborne, *Life and Correspondence of John A. Quitman, Major-General, U. S. A., and Governor of the State of Mississippi* (2 vols., New York, 1860); Oakes, *The Ruling Race*, 223-24, 236-39.

8. Cleo Hearon, "Mississippi and the Compromise of 1850," *PMHS* 14 (1914), 7-229.

9. Arthur E. Jones, Jr., in *HAM* 2: 181-85; Winans to Longstreet, May 27, 1850.

10. Winans to Longstreet, May 27, 1850; to Jefferson Hamilton, Nov. 4, 1850. See William A. Smith, *Lectures on the Philosophy and Practice of Slavery . . .* (Nashville, 1856).

11. Winans to Hamilton, Nov. 4, 1850. See Moses M. Henkle, *The Life of Henry Bidleman Bascom* (Louisville, 1854).

12. Jones, *Methodism* 2: 345-46; James, *Antebellum Natchez*, 247.

13. John J. Tigert, Jr., *Bishop Holland Nimmon McTyeire, Ecclesiastical and Educational Architect* (Nashville, 1955).

14. Winans to Wesley P. Winans, Dec. 15, 1851; Sept. 3, 1852; to Obadiah Winans, Nov. 8, 1852. See James, *Antebellum Natchez*, 285-88; Glover Moore, in *HM* 1: 420-37.

15. Henry S. Foote, *Casket of Reminiscences* (Washington, D. C., 1874); John E. Gonzales, "The Public Career of Henry Stuart Foote (1804-1880)" (Ph. D. dissertation, University of North Carolina, 1957).

16. Cain, *Methodism*, 83-84, citing *Yazoo Democrat*, Jan. 21, 1852.

17. Winans to Wesley P. Winans, Sept. 23, 1853.

18. *NOCA*, Jan. 1, 1850, p. 2.

19. Cain, *Methodism*, 93.

20. Rowland, *Mississippi* 1: 750; Posey, *Old Southwest*, 111; William H. Patton, "History of the Prohibition Movement in Mississippi," *PMHS* 10 (1909), 3-18. Lewis' temperance paper, *The Reformer*, was published in Handsboro. Cain, *Methodism*, 122.

21. W. W. Pinson, *Walter Russell Lambuth, Prophet and Pioneer* (Nashville, 1924), 15-22.

22. Cabaniss, *University of Mississippi*, 30-37.

23. Cain, *Methodism*, 106-07.

24. Pinson, *Lambuth*, 19.

25. *NOCA*, March 25, 1854, p. 2.

26. Smith, *George Foster Pierce*; A. H. Redford, *Life and Times of H. H. Kavanaugh* (Nashville, 1884); *Lives of Methodist Bishops*. Theodore L. Flood and John W. Hamilton, ed. (New York, 1882); Holifield, *Gentlemen Theologians*, 218; Winans to William H. Watkins, June 20, 1856. Pierce maintained that slavery was "a great missionary institution." Quoted in Smith, *In His Image*, 200.

27. Nelson, *Burning Bush and A Flaming Fire*, 67-123. The opening of Whitworth is described in *BHMM* 2: 332-35; Edward Mayes, *History of Education in Mississippi* (Washington, 1899), 56. While delivering his commencement oration at Centenary, Henry D. Berry "refused to look at his manuscript and after a severe and protracted struggle triumphed"! Winans, Journal, Nov. 15, 1854.

28. William Winans, *The Gospel Ministry* (Nashville, 1854); Journal, Nov. 14-15, 1854.

29. *NOCA*, July 30, 1858, p. 1.

30. Winans, Journal, May 2-3, 1857; Winans to Benjamin M. Drake, May 12, 1857.

31. *JGC*, 1858, pp. 416, 586; *The Methodist Discipline* (1844), Section 10, Part 2.

32. Marshall allegedly seethed with "hatred of everything northern." John Hope Franklin, *A Southern Odyssey: Travelers in the Antebellum North* (Baton Rouge, 1976), xv, 75. See William S. Jenkins, *Pro-Slavery Thought in the Old South* (Chapel Hill, 1935).

33. Arthur E. Jones, Jr., in *HAM* 2: 205.

34. Mattison, *The Impending Crisis*, 70. A "majority of Northern Methodists were ready to identify themselves with any political movement which might rid the nation" of slavery. Sweet, *Methodism in American History*, 278.

35. Percy L. Rainwater, "An Analysis of the Secession Controversy in Mississippi, 1854-1861," *Mississippi Valley Historical Review* 24 (June, 1937), 35-42; Robert W. Dubay, *John Jones Pettus, Mississippi Fire-Eater: His Life and Times, 1813-1867* (Jackson, 1979); *Journal of the State Convention and Ordinances and Resolutions Adopted in January, 1861, with An Appendix* (Jackson, 1861), 5.

36. Lillian A. Pereyra, *James Lusk Alcorn, Persistent Whig* (Baton Rouge, 1966).

37. Rowland, *Mississippi* 1: 781-84.

38. *Charleston Mercury*, April 13, 1861, p. 1; *New York Times*, April 13, 1861, p. 1.

39. J. C. Deupree, "The Noxubee Squadron of the First Mississippi Cavalry, C. S. A., 1861-1865," *PMHS*, Centenary Series 2 (1918), 16-18; Davis, *Recollections of Mississippi and Mississippians*, 401-39.

40. James, *Antebellum Natchez*, 281.

41. Cain, *Methodism*, 297.

42. Richard P. Weiner, "The Neglected Key to the Gulf Coast," *JMH* 31 (Oct., 1969), 282-300; Archer Jones, *Confederate Strategy from Shiloh to Vicksburg* (Baton Rouge, 1961).

43. Cain, *Methodism*, 297. During and after World War I Methodism was "more deeply penetrated by pacifism than any other major denomination." Robert Moats Miller, in *HAM* 3: 406.

44. Cain, *Methodism*, 303-04, 317-18.

45. *Ibid.*, 319-24, 331-51.

46. *Jackson Mississippian*, Dec. 6, 1861; Fayette Quarterly Conference Journal, 1861, pp. 296, 319.

47. This was only one chapter in a "tale of ecclesiastical conquest, aided and abetted by the federal government itself." Ralph E. Morrow, *Northern Meth-*

odism and Reconstruction (East Lansing, 1956), 32-33. See William Warren Sweet, *The Methodist Episcopal Church and the Civil War* (Cincinnati, 1912), 96-110.

48. Yankee Bishop Matthew Simpson deemed it a "solemn duty of the Mother Church to send shepherds" to her lost sheep in New Orleans and elsewhere across the South. James W. May, in *HAM* 2: 250, quoting from the *True Delta*, March 28, 1864. See George R. Crooks, *The Life of Bishop Matthew Simpson of the Methodist Episcopal Church* (New York, 1891); Robert D. Clark, *The Life of Matthew Simpson* (New York, 1956).

49. Cain, *Methodism*, 344-45; T. L. Mellen, *Life and Labors of William H. Watkins* (Nashville, 1886).

50. *Western CA*, Aug. 6, 1862, p. 2.

51. Edwin C. Bearss, in *HM* 1: 448-49.

52. Cain, *Methodism*, 352-53.

53. Now freed from their fetters, no increase in black members was reported during 1863-1864. Cain, *Methodism*, 339.

54. Pinson, *Lambuth*, 32-33.

55. *Ibid.*, 33.

56. Thomas D. Clark, *A Pioneer Southern Railroad from New Orleans to Cairo* (Chapel Hill, 1936); Carlton J. Corliss, *Main Line of Mid-America, the Story of the Illinois Central* (New York, 1950).

57. Cain, *Methodism*, 378-98.

58. Henry P. Lewis, Autobiography, 33. Methodist Archives, Millsaps-Wilson Library.

59. Cain, *Methodism*, 393-95.

60. *Ibid.*, 390-91; Ross Henderson Moore, "Social and Economic Conditions in Mississippi during Reconstruction" (Ph. D. dissertation, Duke University, 1938).

61. Hunter D. Farish, *The Circuit Rider Dismounts. A Social History of Southern Methodism, 1865-1900* (Richmond, 1938), 262 *et passim*.

62. *JMC*, 1865, pp. 9-11; Cain, *Methodism*, 400-02.

63. Sandra E. Small, "The Yankee Schoolmarm in Freedmen's Schools: An Analysis of Attitudes,"

Journal of Southern History 45 (Aug., 1979), 381-402.

64. William C. Harris, *Presidential Reconstruction in Mississippi* (Baton Rouge, 1967); *The Day of the Carpetbagger: Republican Reconstruction in Mississippi* (Baton Rouge, 1979); Eric Foner, *Politics and Ideology in the Age of the Civil War* (New York, Oxford, 1980), 97-127.

65. Paul M. Gaston, *The New South Creed: A Study in Southern Mythmaking* (New York, 1970).

66. Richard Irby, *History of Randolph-Macon College* (Richmond, [1899]); Nora C. Chaffin, *Trinity College, 1839-1892: The Beginnings of Duke University* (Durham, 1950); David Duncan Wallace, *History of Wofford College* (Nashville, 1951).

67. Garrett Biblical Institute, Evanston, Illinois, was opened in 1855. Boston University, whose roots were planted at Newbury, Vermont, by Osmon C. Baker and John Dempster thirty years previously, was founded in 1868. Sylvanus M. Duvall, *The Methodist Episcopal Church and Education up to 1869* (New York, 1928), 49-55.

68. *JGC*, 1866, pp. 15-21.

69. *Ibid.*, 135-37.

70. Cain, *Methodism*, 412-13, 417.

71. Cabaniss, *University of Mississippi*, 60-61.

72. Warren A. Candler, *Bishop Charles Betts Galloway: A Prince of Preachers and a Christian Statesman* (Nashville, 1927), 26-27; "Charlie" Galloway to his father, Feb. 23, 1867. Galloway Papers, Millsaps-Wilson Library, Jackson.

73. At "union meetings" on the frontier it was not unusual for seven preachers to address "the listening thousands at the same time" from different pulpit stands. Peter Cartwright, *The Autobiography of Peter Cartwright, the Backwoods Preacher.* W. P. Strickland, ed. (New York, Cincinnati, 1856), 30-31. W. Calvin Wells later (1875) masterminded the Democratic "Mississippi Plan" to "intimidate Negroes if persuasion fails." David G. Sansing, in *HM* 1: 586 citing Wells' article in *PMHS* 9 (1908),

104.

74. Cain, *Methodism*, 452; William L. Duren, *Charles Betts Galloway, Orator, Preacher, and "Prince of Christian Chivalry"* (Atlanta, 1932).

75. Frederick Sullens, in Jackson *Clarion-Ledger Daily News*, May 13, 1909.

76. Farish, *Circuit Rider Dismounts*, 260-72; Nashville *CA*, Aug. 3, 1934, pp. 14-15, reflecting on postwar conditions in church and society.

77. William L. Hamrick, *The Mississippi Conference of the Methodist Protestant Church* (Jackson, 1957), 75-83.

78. *CAJ*, Sept. 21, 1865, p. 1.

79. *JGC*, 1866, p. 50. Laypersons were now authorized to hold official offices in the church and serve as delegates to Methodist conferences.

80. "Fraternal Messengers" were mutually exchanged and "made to feel at home." Cain, *Methodism*, 407.

81. Clifton L. Ganus, Jr., "The Freedman's Bureau in Mississippi" (Ph. D. dissertation, Tulane University, 1953). Methodist Protestants "made history by ordaining two colored deacons: John Faulkner and J. D. Walden." Hamrick, *Mississippi Conference*, 70.

82. Sweet, *Methodism in American History*, 312-13.

83. William C. Harris, "Formulation of the First Mississippi Plan: The Black Code of 1865," *JMH* 29 (May, 1967), 181-201; *JMC*, 1866, pp. 13-14.

84. Miller, *North Mississippi Methodism*, 86; *JMC*, 1867, pp. 14-15; C. H. Phillips, *A History of the Colored Methodist Episcopal Church in America* (Jackson, Tenn., 1900). Cf. Smith, *In His Image*, 230-32.

85. Cain, *Methodism*, 219; Harris, *Presidential Reconstruction*, 36-37, 112, 547-48.

86. Cain, *Methodism*, 454.

87. *Ibid.*, 457, 472.

88. Sweet, *Methodism in American History*, 312-13.

89. One brother described Bishop Vanderhorst as "black enough for any of us," but Bishop Miles was

"bright." Phillips, *Colored Methodist Episcopal Church*, 51, quoting the new paper, *Christian Index*, edited by Samuel Watson.

90. David H. Bradley, Sr., *A History of the A. M. E. Zion Church, 1796-1872* (Nashville, 1956).

Five: Rebuilders of the Battered Breastworks

1. William C. Harris, "A Reconsideration of the Mississippi Scalawag," *JMH* 32 (Feb., 1970), 3-42.

2. *Mississippi Senate Journal*, 1870, p. 48.

3. Charles B. Galloway, *Great Men and Great Movements. A Volume of Addresses* (Nashville, 1914), 146-47.

4. Vernon L. Wharton, *The Negro in Mississippi, 1865-1890* (Chapel Hill, 1947), 159-61; George Alexander Sewell, *Mississippi Black History Makers* (Jackson, 1977), 15-16.

5. Phillips, *Colored Methodist Episcopal Church*, 71-72.

6. *JGC*, 1874, p. 543. See Francis Butler Simkins, *A History of the South* (New York, 1959), 307.

7. Miller, *North Mississippi Methodism*, 96-114; Cain, *Methodism*, 475-76; first issue of *JNMC*, 1871, *passim*.

8. During five decades the Mississippi Conference had given birth and material support to new annual conferences across the Deep South: Alabama, Louisiana, Memphis, Texas and North Mississippi, including two black conferences.

9. William B. Jones, *Methodism in the Mississippi Conference* (Jackson, 1951), 2-5, 272. Distinguished from John G. Jones by the absence of volume citation.

10. Cain, *Methodism*, 443-44.

11. *Ibid.*, 442-48.

12. Jones, *Methodism*, 47; Hamrick, *Mississippi Conference*, 68.

13. Jones, *Methodism*, 10-12, 14, 20-21, 26-37; Mill-

er, *North Mississippi Methodism,* 104.

14. Jones, *Methodism,* 10-12. Church edifices were valued at $270,535, and seven parsonages at $26,150.

15. John H. Moore, "Mississippi's Ante-Bellum Textile Industry," *JMH* 16 (April, 1954), 81-98.

16. Cain, *Methodism,* 442; Rowland, *Mississippi* 2: 714.

17. Jones, *Methodism,* 45-46; John F. Stover, "Colonel Henry S. McComb, Mississippi Railroad Adventurer," *JMH* 17 (April, 1955), 177-90.

18. Jones, *Methodism* 2: 556.

19. J. B. Cain, *Magnolia Methodist Church, 1856-1956* (Nashville, 1956), 34-36.

20. Cain, *Methodism,* 134.

21. Indenture of Trust and Charter, Duke University *Bulletin,* 1926-1927, Part I, vii-ix; Robert F. Durden, *The Dukes of Durham, 1865-1929* (Durham, 1975), 3-10.

22. *JGC,* 1866, pp. 19-20; *Nashville CA,* Jan. 4, 1866, p. 4.

23. Faculty Resolution, May 21, 1861, noting that with only three students remaining, the college would be closed "for the present." Cain, *Methodism,* 298, 464.

24. Cain, *Methodism,* 469. Reed was the son of Senator Thomas B., who died in 1829. Claiborne, *Mississippi,* 358n, 394.

25. Cain, *Methodism,* 465.

26. Jones, *Methodism,* 32-33, 61-62, 95.

27. Edwin Mims, *History of Vanderbilt University* (Nashville, 1946); Landon Cabell Garland, "The Founding of Vanderbilt University," *Nashville CA,* May 24, 1890, p. 10.

28. Bard Thompson, *History of Vanderbilt Divinity School* (Nashville, 1958); Oscar P. Fitzgerald, *Dr. Summers: A Life Study* (Nashville, 1884).

29. Northern Methodists founded their third theological seminary at Madison, New Jersey, in 1867. Ezra S. Tipple, *Drew Theological Seminary, 1867-1917* (New York, Cincinnati, 1917).

30. Farish, *Circuit Rider Dismounts*, 272.

31. Under the presidency of Charles G. Andrews, Centenary was enjoying "better prospects and larger attendance" than ever before. Jones, *Methodism*, 151.

32. *Ibid.*, 121, 273.

33. *Ibid.*, 80. See Frank E. Gaebelein, *Christian Education in a Democracy* (New York, 1951), 212-36.

34. Candler, *Galloway*, 29-32.

35. Jones, *Methodism*, 80.

36. *Ibid.*, 95. See Durden, *Galloway*, 259-77.

37. Richard M. Cameron, in *HAM* 1: 278-87.

38. Jones, *Methodism*, 81.

39. *Ibid.*, 81-82.

40. Stuart G. Noble, *Forty Years of the Public Schools in Mississippi with Special Reference to the Education of the Negro* (New York, 1918); Elise Timberlake, "Did the Reconstruction Regime Give Mississippi Her Public Schools?" *PMHS* 12 (1912), 72-93.

41. Jones, *Methodism*, 165-66.

42. Charles B.Galloway, *The Editor-Bishop: Linus Parker, his Life and Writings* (Nashville, 1886).

43. Jones, *Methodism*, 87.

44. Wesley M. Gewehr, *The Great Awakening in Virginia, 1740-1790* (Durham, 1930).

45. Jones, *Methodism*, 87-88, 108-10, 125.

46. Clement Eaton, *Jefferson Davis* (New York, London, 1977), 14, 44.

47. Jones, *Methodism*, 157. "Many of the old-time camp-meeting grounds were rapidly being transformed into respectable middle-class summer resorts with only a tinge of religion." Sweet, *Methodism in American History*, 333.

48. Jones, *Methodism*, 84, 102, 224.

49. *Ibid.*, 150-51, 164-65; James Cannon, *History of Southern Methodist Missions* (Nashville, 1926); W. Richey Hogg, in *HAM* 3: 59-128.

50. Miss Haygood, sister of Bishop Atticus G., built McTyeire School in Shanghai into "an outstanding institution for Chinese young women." Hogg, in *HAM* 3: 74; Jones, *Methodism*, 157. See Atticus G.

Haygood, *Our Brother in Black: His Freedom and His Future* (New York, 1876).

51. Pinson, *Lambuth*, 35-47; Jones, *Methodism*, 316-17.

52. Henry Steele Commager, *The American Mind. An Interpretation of American Thought and Character Since the 1880's* (New Haven, 1950), 162-95.

53. Jones, *Methodism*, 274-75.

54. David G. Sansing, in *HM* 1: 578.

55. Willie D. Halsell, "The Bourbon Period in Mississippi Politics, 1875-1890," *Journal of Southern History* 11 (Nov., 1945), 519-37; Frank L. Owsley, "The Fundamental Causes of the Civil War: Egocentric Sectionalism," *ibid.* 7 (Aug., 1941), 3-18.

56. Albert D. Kirwan, *Revolt of the Rednecks: Mississippi Politics, 1876-1925* (Lexington, 1951), 1-66; Charles Sallis, "The Color Line in Mississippi Politics, 1865-1915" (Ph. D. dissertation, University of Kentucky, 1967).

57. Sewell, *Black History Makers*, 15-37.

58. Sansing and Waller, *Governor's Mansion*, 77-83; James G. Revels, in *HM* 1: 595-97; Miller, *North Mississippi Methodism*, 105.

59. Revels, in *HM* 1: 597.

60. Jones, *Methodism*, 28.

61. "The Methodism of to-morrow will be distinguished for courageous but cautious statesmanship in legislation." Galloway, *Great Men and Great Movements*, 36.

62. Candler, *Galloway*, 29-32.

63. *NOCA*, April 16, 1874; Sept. 23, 1875; July 20, 1876.

64. C. Vann Woodward, *The Strange Career of Jim Crow* (Third revised edn., New York, 1974), 60-61.

65. Galloway, *Great Men and Great Movements*, 313.

66. Candler, *Galloway*, 68.

67. William G. Davis, "Attacking 'The Matchless Evil:' Temperance and Prohibition in Mississippi, 1817-1908" (Ph. D. dissertation, Mississippi State University, 1975).

68. *The Methodist Discipline* (1844), Chap. I, Sect. 21; (1858), Chap. I, Sec. 4. H. R. Singleton was chairman of the Temperance Committee; T. B. Holloman was secretary. Jones, *Methodism*, 79.

69. Patton, "Prohibition Movement in Mississippi," 181-82, 193; Jones, *Methodism*, 209.

70. Galloway was a rock-ribbed Democrat. Davis, "The 'Matchless Evil,'" 186-99, 206-32; Durden, *Galloway*, 237-55.

71. Candler, *Galloway*, 68.

72. Davis deplored the fact that "a dignitary of the Methodist Church, South, should have left the pulpit and the Bible to mount the political rostrum and plead the higher law of prohibitionism—the substitution of force for free will . . . In this I see the forbidden union of Church and State." Davis to Galloway, Sept. 7, 1887, quoted in Candler, *Galloway*, 213-19.

73. Galloway to Davis, Sept. 23, 1887. Galloway Papers, Millsaps-Wilson Library, Jackson.

74. Sweet, *Methodism in American History*, 356-58; Wilbur Fisk Tillett, "The Value of Theological Education," *Nashville CA*, Aug. 16, 1894, p. 3.

75. Candler, *Galloway*, 78-79. A visitor, who had heard the greatest preachers in the East, declared that the bishop's sermon surpassed "anything" he had "ever heard." See DeRosier, *Removal of the Choctaw Indians*, 129-47.

76. Candler, *Galloway*, 100-70; John R. Mott, *The Student Volunteer Movement for Foreign Missions* (New York, 1946).

77. Candler, *Galloway*, 273-74. Peter James, Jr., the son of a pioneer circuit rider, became "a prosperous planter in the Yazoo delta" and "a liberal supporter of the Methodist Church," including the gift of an observatory to Millsaps College. Cain, *Methodism*, 459.

78. George Washington Gable, in Arlin Turner, ed., *The Negro Question: A Selection of Writings on Civil Rights in the South* . . . (Garden City, 1958), 36.

79. Galloway, *Great Men and Great Movements*, 312-28.

80. *Ibid.*, 316-17, 256. See Woodward, *The Strange Career of Jim Crow*, 67-109; Durden, *Galloway*, 279-301.

81. John S. McNeily, "History of the Measures Submitted to the Committee on Elective Franchise, Apportionments, and Elections in the Constitutional Convention of 1890," *PMHS* 6 (1902), 129-40; Derrick A. Bell, Jr., in Robert Haws, ed., *The Age of Segregation: Race Relations in the South, 1890-1945* (Jackson, 1978), 12-17.

82. James W. Silver, *Mississippi: The Closed Society* (New York, 1963, 1964), 16, quoting J. J. Chrisman.

83. J. Allen Lindsey, *Methodism in the Mississippi Conference* (Jackson, 1964), 8-24, 35-77 *passim*; Jones, *Methodism*, 416-18, 432; Candler, *Galloway*, 171-89.

84. Lindsey, *Methodism*, 25, 56, 64. Hemingway, state treasurer, was currently under indictment for mismanagement of public funds. James P. Coleman, in *HM* 2: 5.

85. *NOCA*, March 1, 1894, p. 4; Jones, *Methodism*, 361, 455-56; Lindsey, *Methodism*, 275-76; Candler, *Galloway*, 260-65; Durden, *Galloway*, 297-99.

86. Durden, *Galloway*, 262-64. Board members included Lieutenant-Governor Garvin Dugas Shands. Jones, *Methodism*, 386-87. Shands was the first official dean of the university law school, 1897. Frank E. Everett, Jr., in *HM* 2: 380.

Six: Crusaders for Christ and Democracy

1. Key, "Historical Sketch," 6-8. Ninety years later it was affirmed that Millsaps "will continue to endeavor to serve the Church in the ministry of teaching within the framework of a Christian philosophy of education." *JMC*, 1980, p. 137.

2. Commager, *The American Mind*, 41-54; Galloway, *Great Men and Great Movements*, 236.

3. Jones, *Methodism*, 456-57; Lindsey, *Methodism*,

23, 33, 37, 65-66, 76.

4. Galloway, *Great Men and Great Movements*, 227-37.

5. Jackson *Clarion-Ledger*, June 4, 1903, p. 1. "A major turning point in the cultural life of Mississippi was the Spanish-American War," the beginning of a movement of the state "back into the mainstream" of national life. Joseph C. Kiger, in *HM* 2: 492.

6. Galloway, *Great Men and Great Movements*, 119-47.

7. Dallas C. Dickey, *Seargent S. Prentiss: Whig Orator of the Old South* (Baton Rouge, 1945).

8. Galloway, *Great Men and Great Movements*, 122-26.

9. Lindsey, *Methodism*, 84, 99.

10. William F. Holmes, *The White Chief, James Kimble Vardaman* (Baton Rouge, 1970), 101-15; George C. Osborn, *James Kimble Vardaman: Southern Commoner* (Jackson, 1981); Eugene E. White, "Anti-Racial Agitation in Politics: James Kimble Vardaman in the Mississippi Gubernatorial Campaign of 1903," *JMH* 7 (Jan., 1945), 91-110.

11. Galloway, *Great Men and Great Movements*, 316. Vardaman may have assumed that when Galloway "elaborated his racial theory in concrete terms, he revealed his firm adherence to the dogma of Negro inferiority." Smith, *In His Image*, 283.

12. Galloway, *Great Men and Great Movements*, 138-41.

13. *Ibid.*, 236.

14. Editorial in the Jackson *Daily News*, May 13, 1909.

15. Lindsey, *Methodism*, 89-90, 139-40, 174, 191-92, 312-13; Rowland, *Mississippi* 2: 502-03; Nollie W. Hickman, in *HM* 2: 218-22; Frank Everett, Jr., *ibid.* 2: 381; Key, "Historical Sketch," 6-11.

16. Faculty listings, Millsaps College *Bulletin*, 1900-1920.

17. Lindsey, *Methodism*, 247.

18. Holmes, *Vardaman*, 87-88.

19. C. H. Buchanan, in *Nashville CA*, Jan. 30, 1902, p. 4; May 15, 1902, p. 2.

20. *State of Tennessee, ex. rel., vs. Board of Trust of Vanderbilt University, et. al.*, 129 Tennessee 289 (Columbia, Mo., 1914); *Nashville CA*, March 27, 1914, pp. 4-5, 16-J, 16-K.

21. *Nashville CA*, Aug. 28, 1914, pp. 10-11. See Paul N. Garber, *John Carlisle Kilgo* (Durham, 1937).

22. *JGC*, 1914, pp. 45-51, 79-80, 198, 489-92; *Nashville CA*, May 8, 1914, pp. 3-16; July 24, 1914, pp. 3-5.

23. *History of the North Texas Conference and the Dallas District* . . . (Dallas, 1925), 24-25; *Nashville CA*, Aug. 28, 1914, pp. 10-11; July 9, 1915, pp. 5, 9; Olin W. Nail, *Texas Methodism, 1900-1960* (Austin, 1961).

24. William Preston Few, in an address before the Twentieth Century Club, Boston, in 1927. *Nashville CA*, July 15, 1927, p. 18; *North Carolina CA*, July 7, 1927, p. 1.

25. Bishop Hoss declared that the church would not "for one day consent to educate her ministers in an atmosphere of an alien university." *Nashville CA*, Aug. 28, 1914, p. 12. Henry Nelson Snyder was convinced that Methodism "tossed away in a fever of blinding emotionalism the richest opportunity for educational service ever given to an ecclesiastical body in the South." *An Educational Odyssey* (New York, 1947), 194-95.

26. Lindsey, *Methodism*, 228, 241, 250.

27. *Ibid.*, 210, 221, 232, 233, 248-49.

28. *NOCA*, Sept. 2, 1915. Special edition on Whitworth.

29. Lindsey, *Methodism*, 231, 271, 275-76.

30. Francis Asbury, *Journal*, Jan. 5, 1796; Sweet, *Methodism in American History*, 208; Richard M. Cameron, in *HAM* 1: 266-68.

31. Lindsey, *Methodism*, 177-78, 208-09, 247-48.

32. *Ibid.*, 151, 187-203, 209, 219, 248, 295.

33. *Ibid.*, 191, 206-07, 217, 245; *MMA*, Dec. 2, 1959. Scarritt, founded at Kansas City in 1892 by Belle

Harris Bennett and others, was moved to Nashville and associated with Vanderbilt in 1924. W. Richey Hogg, in *HAM* 3: 71.

34. Alfred M. Pierce, *Giant Against the Sky: The Life of Bishop Warren Akin Candler* (New York, Nashville, 1948).

35. Lindsey, *Methodism*, 301.

36. R. A. Meek quoted. *Ibid.*

37. *Ibid.*, 266.

38. Over $140,000,000 was raised for home and foreign missions. *Daily CA*, May 10, 1926, p. 39.

39. Lindsey, *Methodism*, 292-94.

40. *Ibid.*, 292-93, 305; Pinson, *Lambuth*, 198.

41. Lindsey, *Methodism*, 287; A. Wigfall Green, *The Man Bilbo* (Baton Rouge, 1963).

42. Lindsey, *Methodism*, 283, 289.

43. Green, *Bilbo*, 61.

44. Lindsey, *Methodism*, 287, 300-01, 312-13.

45. *Ibid.*, 297-98; Rowland, *Mississippi* 2: 363-81.

46. Lindsey, *Methodism*, 297-98.

47. Rowland, *Mississippi* 2: 383-90.

48. *Ibid.*, 2: 377.

49. The judge warned of possible adverse results from the effort "to limit Negro suffrage." James P. Coleman, in *HM* 2: 5-6.

50. Pinson, *Lambuth*, 177-79.

51. *Ibid.*, 177-78.

52. Lambuth to E. O. Watson, Oct. 15, 1918, quoted *ibid.*, 178.

53. "For southern whites, the commitment to the use of force to maintain the southern system was as frequent and determined as manifestations of discontent and insubordination towards the system on the part of black southerners." Al-Tony Gilmore, in Haws, *Age of Segregation*, 76.

54. Green, *Bilbo*, 62n.

55. Pinson, *Lambuth*, 180-81.

56. *Ibid.*, 179.

57. *Ibid.*, 288, 305-06.

58. In October of 1919 some $200,000 worth of

automobiles were parked in the shade during camp meeting at New Prospect. Lindsey, *Methodism*, 310. One year later the price of cotton had plummeted, debts were mounting, and bank accounts were rapidly dwindling. William D. McCain, in *HM* 2: 73-78.

59. K. E. Barnhart, "The Evolution of the Social Consciousness of Methodism" (Ph.D. dissertation, University of Chicago, 1924); Henry Y. Warnock, "Andrew Sledd, Southern Methodists, and the Negro," *Journal of Southern History*, 31 (Aug., 1965), 251-71.

60. Kenneth T. Jackson, *The Ku Klux Klan in the City, 1915-1930* (New York, 1967), 237.

61. *NOCA*, April 28; May 21; July 28, 1921, pp. 1, 2.

62. *JMC*, 1925, pp. 83-84; Frederick E. Maser, in *HAM* 3: 450-51.

63. *JMC*, 1925, pp. 83-84; Clayton Rand, *Ink on My Hands* (Gulfport, 1940), 225-41.

64. *JMC*, 1925, pp. 83-84.

65. Author's conversation with J. B. Cain, May 1976.

66. *Nashville CA*, Jan. 21, 1921, p. 69.

67. Miller, *North Mississippi Methodism*, 106.

68. *JMC*, 1926, p. 84.

69. William J. McCutcheon, in *HAM* 3: 261.

70. *JMC*, 1925, p. 81.

71. *Laws of the State of Mississippi*, 1926, p. 435; Bill R. Baker, *Catch the Vision. The Life of Henry L. Whitfield of Mississippi* (Jackson, 1974).

72. S. J. Simon, *John Wesley and the Religious Societies* (London, 1921); Umphrey Lee, *John Wesley and Modern Religion* (Nashville, 1936).

73. *JMC*, 1925, pp. 74-75; *MMA*, Dec. 2, 1959, p. 11.

74. *JMC*, 1925, p. 53; 1929, pp. 90-91; 1930, p. 54. See McLemore, *Mississippi Baptists*, 261-62.

75. *JMC*, 1925, pp. 90-92; 1927, pp. 66-67; 1929, pp. 67-72. See Richard A. McLemore, in *HM* 2: 418.

76. *MMA*, Dec. 2, 1959, pp. 17-20; *JMC*, 1925, p. 95; 1928, pp. 73-74; 1938, pp. 95-96.

77. Donald B. Kelley, "Deep South Dilemma: The Mississippi Press in the Presidential Election of 1928," *JMH* 25 (Feb., 1963), 63-92.

78. Robert Moats Miller, in *HAM* 3: 357-59.

79. *NOCA*, May 10, 1928, p. 2; Virginius Dabney, *Dry Messiah: The Life of Bishop Cannon* (New York, 1949), 180-88; James Cannon, Jr., *Bishop Cannon's Own Story*. Richard L. Watson, ed. (Durham, 1955), 391-447.

80. *NOCA*, May 10, 1928, p. 2; July 5, 26; Aug. 16, 30, 1928, p. 1. See Edwin A. Moore, *A Catholic Runs for President: The Campaign of 1928* (New York, 1956); Kenneth K. Bailey, *Southern White Protestantism in the Twentieth Century* (New York, 1964), 92-100.

81. Green, *Bilbo*, 77-78.

82. Author's recollection as an impressionable freshman with a shaved head and purple "beanie."

83. Smith, *In His Image*, 283-84.

84. The bishop apparently declared out of order any motion suggesting "integration." *JMC*, 1926, pp. 27 ff; 1927, pp. 29 ff; 1928, pp. 28 ff; *Nashville CA*, Nov. 4, 1927, pp. 9-10; Nov. 9, 1928, pp. 6-7.

Seven: Reconcilers of A People Under God

1. Richard Kluger, *Simple Justice: The History of Brown v. Board of Education and Black America's Struggle for Equality* (New York, 1976).

2. Lindsey, *Methodism*, 219.

3. Winans, Autobiography, 119.

4. Paul H. Conkin, *FDR and the Origins of the Welfare State* (New York, 1967); Robert S. McElvaine, ed., *Down & Out in the Great Depression: Letters of the Forgotten Man* (Chapel Hill, 1982).

5. Annie K. Jackson, "The Political Rise of Martin Sennett Conner" (M. A. thesis, Mississippi State University, 1950).

6. Martha H. Swain, *Pat Harrison. The New Deal Years* (Jackson, 1978), 26-27; Lindsey, *Methodism,* 277; Kirwan, *Revolt of the Rednecks,* 271-72.

7. Jackson *Daily News,* Jan. 9, 1930; Jan. 21, 1932; *JMC,* 1931, pp. 28, 33.

8. *JMC,* 1931, p. 56.

9. *Ibid.*

10. *Ibid.,* 62.

11. May 7, 1932.

12. William Winter, "Governor Mike Conner and the Sales Tax, 1932," *JMH* 41 (Aug., 1979), 213-30.

13. *JMC,* 1932, p. 39.

14. Dixon Wecter, *The Age of Depression—1929-1941* (New York, 1948), 66; Robert Bendiner, *Just Around the Corner: A Highly Selected History of the Thirties* (New York, 1967), 32-35.

15. *JMC,* 1934, pp. 43-44.

16. *Ibid.,* 62-65; *Nashville CA,* Oct. 13, 20, 1933, pp. 1296, 1318 continuous pagination.

17. *JMC,* 1934, p. 65.

18. *Ibid.,* 77.

19. *Ibid.,* 77-78.

20. William J. McCutcheon, "Theology of the Methodist Episcopal Church During the Interwar Period, 1919-1939" (Ph. D. dissertation, Yale University, 1960).

21. In 1937 members of the American Student Union at Millsaps petitioned Senator Bilbo to endorse the Gavagan anti-lynching bill before the Congress. He "branded the organization communistic and demanded an investigation of all Mississippi student organizations." Swain, *Pat Harrison,* 202.

22. During the Panic of 1837 appeals for offerings for destitute "toiling itinerants" had been so successful that John G. Jones exclaimed: "Up to that date we had met with no such liberality"! Jones, *Methodism* 2: 402.

23. J. Oliver Emmerich, in *HM* 2: 110-19; Jack E. Prince, "History and Development of the Mississippi Balance Agriculture with Industry Program, 1936-

1958" (Ph. D. dissertation, Ohio State University, 1961).

24. *JMC*, 1935, pp. 54, 68.

25. Bishop Candler, quoted in Garber, *One People*, 121.

26. "Mississippi's negative image, and the source of much of its shame, stemmed from the history of race relations in the state." David J. Bodenhamer, in Peggy W. Prenshaw and Jesse O. McKee, ed., *Sense of Place: Mississippi* (Jackson, 1979), 59.

27. *JMC*, 1936, p. 63.

28. *Ibid.*, 104; 1939, pp. 202-08.

29. *Ibid.*, 1948, pp. 165-73. Methodism would "languish" and "die if our educated young preachers prove to lack the essentials of faith and power to turn the times into the ways of Him who is the truth." *Nashville CA*, June 18, 1926, p. 5.

30. In a message to the Northern Methodists in 1876, the aging Lovick Pierce exclaimed that "there is but *one* Episcopal Methodism!" *JGC*, 1876, p. 418.

31. *JMC*, 1937, pp. 36, 62-64.

32. In 1925 the Mississippi Conference rejected the Plan of Union by a vote of 170 to 45; North Mississippi voted 125 to 117 against the plan. In both instances every yea vote was cast by preachers, but laypersons unanimously opposed Unification. *JMC*, 1925, pp. 33-35; *JNMC*, 1925, pp. 30-31.

33. J. Oliver Emmerich, in *HM* 2: 119; *JMC*, 1938, pp. 73-96. A standing vote of 184 yeas and 45 nays approved the Plan of Union. *JMC*, 1937, pp. 39-40.

34. Frederick E. Maser, in *HAM* 3: 455-56. The Methodist Protestants approved the plan by a vote of 142 to 39. Hamrick, *Mississippi Conference*, 293-94.

35. *Journal of the Uniting Conference* (Published by the conference, 1939); Garber, *One People*, 132-40; Maser, in *HAM* 3: 457-76.

36. The plan gave "the Negro more than he had had and made it possible for him to take still more." Francis J. McConnell, in *Zion's Herald*, March 4, 1936, p. 221. See Francis J. McConnell, *The Essentials of*

Methodism (New York, 1916); *Borden Parker Bowne. His Life and His Philosophy* (New York, 1929), 88, 93.

37. Maser, in *HM* 3; 456; *JMC*, 1938, pp. 45-49, 83.

38. *JMC*, 1939, p. 140.

39. John Ray Skates, Jr., in *HM* 2: 120-29.

40. *JMC*, 1940, pp. 89, 96.

41. *Ibid.*, 1941, pp. 92-95.

42. Robert Moats Miller, in *HAM* 3: 406.

43. *JMC*, 1941, pp. 93-95.

44. *Hattiesburg American*, Oct. 8, 11; Nov. 5, 1940.

45. *JMC*, 1942, p. 45.

46. *Ibid.*, 1945, pp. 24-28.

47. *Ibid.*, Special Session, 1945, pp. 32-34.

48. Robert L. Ezelle, Jackson layman and businessman, initiated the project. *JMC*, 1943, p. 47; 1944, p. 39.

49. *Ibid.*, 1944, pp. 96-97.

50. *Ibid.*, 1945, p. 38; *Daily CA*, May 2, 1944, p. 25.

51. *JMC*, 1945, pp. vi, 41, italics omitted. Bailey and Decell were graduates of Millsaps. The governor's administration, cut short by his death, was "a landmark" in the state's educational history. John Ray Skates, in *HM* 2: 132; Jackson *Clarion-Ledger*, Nov. 3, 1946. See J. Oliver Emmerich, *Two Faces of Janus. The Saga of Deep South Change* (Jackson, 1973), 69-70.

52. *JMC*, 1946, pp. 142-43.

53. *Ibid.*, 1947, p. 87; W. Richey Hogg, in *HAM* 1: 118.

54. *JMC*, 1947, p. 126.

55. *Ibid.*, 1948, pp. iv, 42-43; *MMA*, Dec. 2, 1959, pp. 4, 5; Murray H. Leiffer, in *HAM* 5: 518-20.

56. *JMC*, 1948, pp. iv, 42-43, 110-12.

57. *Ibid.*, pp. 110-12; Rush Glenn Miller, ed., "A Guide to the Contents of the Mississippi United Methodist Advocate, 1947-1974" (Jackson, 1974).

58. *JMC*, 1950, pp. 109-10.

59. Cain, *Methodism*, 156, 171; Hawkins, *Methodism in Natchez*, 17-94; Pinson, *Lambuth*, 18-19; Jones, *Methodism* 1: 25-62 *passim*.

60. Pinson, *Lambuth*, 48.

61. *JMC*, 1950, p. 110.

62. *Ibid.; Daily CA*, April 28, 1960, p. 43.

63. Murray H. Leiffer, in *HAM* 3: 485-92; Willis J. Weatherford, *American Churches and the Negro* (Boston, 1957).

64. *JMC*, 1945, p. 43.

65. *Ibid.*, 1943, p. 99.

66. Derrick A. Bell, Jr., in Haws, *Age of Segregation*, 12-17. See Siloiam C. Berman, *The Politics of Civil Rights in the Truman Administration* (Columbus, O., 1970).

67. *Time*, July 1, 1946, p. 23.

68. Author's conversation with T. Edward Hightower, May 7, 1978.

69. *JMC*, 1948, p. 114.

70. John Ray Skates, Jr., in *HM* 2: 132

71. Robert Higgs, in Haws, *Age of Segregation*, 89-116.

72. Elbert R. Hilliard, "A Biography of Fielding Wright: Mississippi's Mr. State Rights" (M. A. thesis, Mississippi State University, 1959).

73. House *Journal*, 1948, p. 85.

74. Emmerich, *Two Faces of Janus*, 87-103; Numan W. Bartley, *The Rise of Massive Resistance: Race and Politics in the South during the 1950's* (Baton Rouge, 1960); Richard C. Ethridge, "Mississippi's Role in the Dixiecrat Movement" (Ph. D. dissertation, Mississippi State University, 1971).

75. William Winter, in *HM* 2: 141-43.

76. Hodding Carter, *The South Strikes Back* (Garden City, 1959).

77. Emmerich, *Two Faces of Janus*, 82-83.

78. Silver, *The Closed Society*, 87-88.

79. *JMC*, 1951, pp. 51, 114-15.

80. *Ibid.*, p. 114.

81. Robert Moats Miller, in *HAM* 3: 405-06.

82. The General Conference was petitioned to "take whatever action is necessary" to require the federation "to drop the word *Methodist* from its

name." *JGC*, 1951, pp. 114-15; *Daily CA*, April 28, 1960, p. 43.

83. Murray H. Leiffer, in *HAM* 3: 494.

84. A Commission on Interjurisdictional Relations was created to continue efforts to abolish the black jurisdiction, promote the spirit of Christian brotherhood and reconciliation, and "achieve a more inclusive church." *The Methodist Discipline*, 1960, Paragraph 2013, Part 1.

Eight: Strategists for the Ideological Wars

1. Albert P. Blaustein and Clarence Clyde Ferguson, Jr., *Desegregation and the Law: The Meaning and Effect of the School Segregation Cases* (Revised edn., New York, 1962); M. Lytle Clifford, *The Warren Court and Its Critics* (Tucson, 1968); Bartley, *Rise of Massive Resistance*, 67; Jackson *Daily News*, Sept. 7, 1954.

2. Rowland, *Mississippi* 2: 293-94.

3. Frederick E. Maser, in *HAM* 3: 451.

4. Silver, *The Closed Society*, 88.

5. Editorial in Jackson *Daily News*, May 18, 1954.

6. *MMA*, Feb. 9, 1954, p. 5; Aug. 25, 1954, pp. 11-13; Dec. 6, 22, 1954, p. 3.

7. *JMC*, 1955, p. 99, leaving "other" open to interpretation.

8. Leon Miller, in Allen Weinstein and Frank Otto Gatell, ed., *The Segregation Era, 1863-1954* (New York, London, 1970), 284.

9. Author's several conversations with Robert Ezelle, September-October 1977.

10. *JMC*, 1959, p. 101.

11. *Ibid.*, 131-33; Neil R. McMillen, in *HM* 2: 158.

12. Asbury was familiarly known as the young Republic's "first Commissioner of Education." Stephen Montford Vail, *Ministerial Education in the Methodist Episcopal Church* (Boston, 1853), 215.

13. Mississippi Methodists deplored "all efforts at regimentation," but they renounced "all efforts

which are designed to inflame the emotions and to feed the flame of racial prejudice." *JMC*, 1959, pp. 131-33.

14. Neil R. McMillen, *The Citizens' Council: Organized Resistance to the Second Reconstruction, 1954-1964* (Urbana, 1971); McMillen, in *HM* 2: 159.

15. Jack Winton Gunn, in *HM* 2: 485.

16. McMillen, in *HM* 2: 159.

17. *JMC*, 1960, p. 149.

18. *MMA*, April 1, 22, 29, 1964, p. 3.

19. *JMC*, 1960, pp. 148-49. Author's conversation with William J. Cunningham during an autograph party, April 28, 1980.

20. Finger apparently resisted the idea of establishing a Methodist theological seminary in Jackson because of its alleged association with the leadership of the Citizens' Council. Author's conversation with Clyde C. Clark, May 5, 1970; *JMC*, 1955, pp. 46, 58, 63, 102.

21. *JMC*, 1960, pp. 148-49; McMillen, in *HM* 2: 155.

22. *JMC*, 1960, p. 148.

23. Emmerich, *Two Faces of Janus*, 131-42. See Reed Sarratt, *The Ordeal of Desegregation: The First Decade* (New York, 1968); Murray H. Leiffer, in *HAM* 3: 552-56.

24. *JMC*, 1960, pp. 148-49; Len Holt, *The Summer that Didn't End* (New York, 1965).

25. Silver, *The Closed Society*, 114-33; James Meredith, *Three Years in Mississippi* (Bloomington, 1966).

26. Silver, *The Closed Society*, 29-30; Cleveland Donald, Jr., in Wells and Cole, *Mississippi Heroes*, 217-28; *MMA*, June 19, 1963, p. 3.

27. William Bradford Huie, *Three Lives for Mississippi* (New York, 1968); *MMA*, June 24, 1964, p. 3.

28. Lester A. Sobel, ed., *Civil Rights, 1960-1966* (New York, 1967); Allan Wolk, *The Presidency and Black Civil Rights: Eisenhower to Nixon* (Rutherford, N. J., 1971); McMillen, in *HM* 2:155-76; author's conversation with Mack B. Stokes, September 8, 1978.

29. *MMA*, Feb. 15, 1961, p. 9.

30. *Ibid.*, 1962, pp. 132-33.

31. McMillen, in *HM* 2: 160-61n.

32. The FBI, the Elks, the Lutherans, the Red Cross, and Jewish War Veterans were also objects of the commission's surveillance. Silver, *The Closed Society*, 40.

33. *JMC*, 1963, pp. 76, 84, 92; 1964, p. 86. Most seminary graduates simply "gave up" on the equivocal racial posture of conference "kingmakers," but Clay Foster Lee, Jr., and others felt compelled to "stay with the ship" and "work out the problem at home." Author's several talks with Loyce Cain McKenzie and Laura Drake Satterfield Sturdivant in late September 1978.

34. *JMC*, pp. 152-53.

35. Silver, *The Closed Society*, 59.

36. W. J. Cunningham, *Agony at Galloway. One Church's Struggle with Social Change* (Jackson, 1980), 141.

37. *JMC*, 1963, p. 84.

38. John C. Satterfield and Loyd Wright, *Blueprint for Total Federal Regimentation: Analysis of the Civil Rights Act of 1963* (Washington, 1963). An alumnus of Millsaps, Satterfield was "Founders Day Speaker" on February 9, 1961, and "Honored for Service" by Bishop Mack B. Stokes in November 1972. *MMA*, Feb. 3, 1961, p. 3; Nov. 22, 1972, p. 4.

39. *MMA*, April 1, 22, 29, 1964, p. 3.

40. *Ibid.*, July 15, 29, 1964, pp. 1, 3.

41. Sansing and Waller, *Governor's Mansion*, 166; Jackson *Daily News*, Jan. 22, 1964.

42. *JMC*, 1964, pp. 116-18.

43. Cunningham, *Agony at Galloway*, 115-16, 139.

44. McMillen, in *HM* 2:164.

45. *JMC*, 1965, p. 116; author's informal chat with Paul B. Johnson, Jr., at deer camp in November 1969.

46. Author's conversation with J. B. Cain in October 1969; telephone conversation with William

D. Mounger in September 1977; Cunningham, *Agony at Galloway*, 88-94.

47. Information provided by Paul Hardin, dean and registrar of Millsaps College, May 1978.

48. Prior to the admission of the black students, the official position of the board of trustees clearly stated that "Segregation always has been, and is now the policy of Millsaps College." Board Minutes, March 18, 1958. In 1964 the board refused to fund a new dormitory with the assistance of the Federal Housing and Finance Agency. *MMA*, Feb. 20, 1964, p. 2; *JMC*, 1965, p. 79.

49. *JMC*, 1963, pp. 120-21.

50. *Ibid.*, 1966, pp. 85, 87-88, 134-35.

51. *Ibid.*, 89. Three years previously, a Tougaloo student named Cleveland Page had been granted permission by the pastor, W. J. Cunningham, to practice on the pipe organ. Fearing for his "physical safety," the young man was "protected" by Mrs. Paul Arrington and Clarice Campbell. Cunningham, *Agony at Galloway*, 22-23.

52. *JMC*, 1966, p. 89.

53. *Ibid.*, 1968, pp. 101-02.

54. Silver, *The Closed Society*, 58.

55. *JMC*, 1968, p. 93; *MMA*, June 16, 1971, p. 1.

56. Jackson *Daily News*, May 14, 1980.

57. *JMC*, 1970, pp. 116-26, 155-61.

58. For developments in agriculture, manufacturing, forest lands, education, health services, cultural and religious affairs in the state from the 1950s to the 1970s, see *HM* 2: 140-569.

59. Joseph C. Kiger, in *HM* 2: 493; Holifield, *Gentlemen Theologians*, 135-36, 139-45.

60. Author's conversation with William P. Davis, executive director of the conference, on February 7, 1980. A conference brochure points out that "MRLC has given to Mississippi the unique distinction of being the first state in the Union to have a religious conference along such broad lines as to involve all religious faiths."

61. Candler, *Galloway*, 171-89.

62. Arthur Bruce Moss, in *HAM* 1: 115-20.

63. *JMC*, 1972, frontispiece.

64. "It cannot be that the people should grow in grace unless they give themselves to reading. A reading people will always be a knowing people." John Wesley to George Holder, Nov. 8, 1790, quoted in *HAM* 1: 24.

65. Galloway, *Great Men and Great Movements*, 236.

66. Jackson *Daily News*, Sept. 20, 1974.

67. *MMA*, June 16, 1971, p. 1; Jackson *Clarion-Ledger Daily News*, May 24, 1980, special section.

68. Jackson *Daily News*, May 5, 1979.

69. Phyl Garland, "A Taste of Triumph for Black Mississippi," *Ebony*, Feb. 1968, pp. 25-32; Jason Berry, *Amazing Grace. With Charles Evers in Mississippi* (New York, 1978).

70. Jackson *Daily News*, March 18, 1978.

71. *JMC*, 1980, p. 119.

72. *Ibid.*, 1980, pp. 82-83.

73. Benjamin Tefft, *Methodism Successful* (New York, 1860), 385.

74. Holifield, *Gentlemen Theologians*, 143.

75. James M. Thoburn, *My Missionary Apprenticeship* (New York, 1886), 112; Clark, *Life of Matthew Simpson*, 224-29.

76. Vail, *Ministerial Education*, 215. See Frank Baker, *From Wesley to Asbury. Studies in Early American Methodism* (Durham, 1976).

77. Winans, Autobiography, 130-31; Claiborne, *Mississippi*, 352-58.

78. Jackson *Clarion-Ledger Daily News*, Jan. 28, 1980, "The Inauguration of Mississippi's 58th Governor."

79. First Baptist Church and Saint Peter's Cathedral also face the Capitol grounds.

80. Robertson, *American Myth, American Reality*, 17.

81. Foner, *Politics and Ideology*, 11-12.

Index of Persons

212